SASKIA

by Jacques Horringa

Published by

The Svengali Press

2, 2-4 Notts Avenue
Bondi Beach,
NSW 2026
AUSTRALIA
trilby@svengalipress.com.au
www.svengalipress.com.au

ISBN 978-0-9946155-4-1 pbk

ISBN 978-1-925706-86-4 ebk

Cover Illustration by Serena Agius

Contents

Dedication

I dedicate this novel to the memory of my
loving wife, Margaret.

Acknowledgements

I was fortunate to have found Marsha Lake from Marsha Lake Secretarial Services who, after typing up my novel, *Saskia*, worked tirelessly to have it published for me. My sincere thanks Marsha.

I would like to thank Inspector of Police (Forensic) David Forbes who sorted out the Police matters in the book.

And last but not least I would like to thank my friends in the Writer's Group, the Waratahs, for their support and advice.

PROLOGUE

SASKIA'S DIARY

24.9.2011

I really fell for him. I wonder if he is married, will I tell him that I work as an escort? May be not. I was never involved romantically. Anyway, now I am living here I will close off much of that part of my life and I will begin the next stage and this time men will only be a small part of that life and then only on my terms. Also, now I have the money I wanted to travel, see the world.

Well, these were my thoughts when I left the agency and moved into my new home. Then HE came into my life!

27.9.2011

He came and he will be back. He promised. This is a new experience for me. Is what I feel for him love? Am I in love? Does he love me? He is so loving and kind. Can this be true? My deepest, my most fervent hope is that if he ever found out about my past it would not bother him. That is the past and our life together will start now.

28.9.2011

I went to see my old mates at the agency. They want me to come back, telling me I look as good and sexy as I was when I started and that is now 17 years ago. Flatterers! I am not going back. I have found my man. Alan was with me again this evening. It was so beautiful I wanted it to go on and on and on. But always he leaves. It hurts and I am lonely when he is gone. Why can't he stay? He's married, that's why. But I don't care. One day, I know, he'll be mine. (I have a suspicion. I don't want to pry, the uncertainty is killing me).

SASKIA

30.9.2011

Alan told me last night that his office is in North Sydney. It is not that far away but the evening traffic is unpredictable so he will be late sometimes. There is not much happening in my life now, but now I have a purpose. Most days I seem to be thinking about the same thing; the fulfilment of my dream of our life together. I pray daily that it will happen soon. I want to wake up in the morning to feel him by my side. One day I will ask him if he is married. I must. But for now that can wait. Will I at last have found happiness and security?

5.10.2011

Alan was again with me last night. He left again but I know one day he will stay and we will be together. I am happy, happier than I've ever been. I am glad I made the decision to leave the small country town I grew up in. I still remember the day I decided to leave my family and go to Sydney, the big city, where it was all happening. The town seemed to have come to a standstill. There was nothing for me there, an ambitious 21-year-old girl dreaming of high- powered jobs in business and finance. I'm good at maths and, I've been told, I'm pretty. Poor, naïve, innocent me thought I just had to show up and people would take me on. Of course it was not like that and my savings quickly dwindled.

I went to the bank and I had to go to a teller because I didn't have a credit card. I never applied for one and I wasn't going to until I had a job. And that is where I met this girl. Glamorous, smartly dressed and confidence oozing out of her. We were in a slow-moving queue in the bank and the long wait was clearly annoying her. She was tapping her foot and sighing. Being a country girl where everybody talks to everybody else, I said: "Yes, it's a bit slow-moving isn't it?" She looked at me, probably wondering if she should ignore me, but then she said: "You look a bit glum, problems?" I hesitated.

Should I tell her? Confide in her? But I was very down, desperate really. I didn't have much money left. By my calculations a bit more than $50, after I had paid the rent.

And then there were my living expenses.

If by the end of the week I still had no job I would have to leave the dump where I live presently and go to …….. I really didn't want to think about that. Anyway, even if she couldn't help me, it would be good to talk to somebody. At least she seemed sympathetic. So, I began telling her my story as we progressed in the queue. When she was called to a teller she said: "Meet me in half an hour in the post office café in Martin Place. You know where it is?" I nodded. I had been there before, not long after arriving in Sydney, still full of high hopes. Although I had some doubts about her coming I went to the café. She came, ordered coffees and asked if I wanted something to eat. I was hungry. To save money I had cut down on my meals and this morning's breakfast had been a cup of coffee.

Anyway I said "Yes" and ate a hearty lunch. Then she offered me a job of being an escort. "You've got a good figure, nice legs which is important in our business. What we do is entertain and, in a way, be entertained. Anyway, if you're interested come and have a chat to us at the agency."

Well, when they explained it all a bit more it made me think. This was not why I had come to Sydney, but, I was broke. The prospects of the jobs I had been dreaming of seemed impossible to get. Maybe I had set my sights too high. And this, well, it was a job. I just couldn't go back home and admit defeat. And, I thought, I don't have to do this forever, just get me back on my feet. Famous last words. It's been 17 years; I am 38 now and finally got the will to say to myself 'enough is enough.' One thing they had a bit of a problem with and that was my name. So I became Saskia, exotic, foreign.

Sounded good to me.

I have written this down for Alan, not as an excuse but as an explanation as to how and why I came to work as an escort.

SASKIA

Because if he found out and is uncomfortable with it; I will give him this to read and hope that it will make him understand.

CHAPTER 1

Alan Henderson looked at his watch – 6.30pm. Time to phone Emma. He shut down the computer and, picking up the phone, punched in his home number. As he waited he swivelled in his chair looking around his office, pleased. He was glad now that at the urging of Liza, his secretary, he had gone ahead and put in new furniture, modern but not too avant garde. The chairs were comfortable. Clients, sipping their coffee, had told him so. They contrasted with the large antique green-leather-topped desk he was sitting at. He had not wanted to part with that. Alan smiled as he recalled his secretary's repeated efforts to sell it and –

"Oh, Emma! Er, yes I'm fine. How are you? Look, I'm sorry to do this to you again but I've got to go to this meeting."

Annoyance crossed his face when he heard the desperation in her voice as she pleaded: "Does it have to be this evening, Alan? You know we – I mean, can't you put it off till tomorrow?"

"No, I can't. I'm sorry but I can't." Irritably he raised his voice at having to defend his decision. Alan added: "Don't you think I'd much rather come home?"

There was a short silence. "I'll keep something warm."

"No, don't. I'll grab something before the meeting. Please don't worry. I'll probably be home around 10, maybe a bit later. It'll depend on the traffic. Now, Emma, he added, softening his voice: "don't wait up. Go to bed."

Another short silence: "Yes, OK. Be careful, darling."
"Yes I will. Bye now."

After the phone call Alan sat for a few moments staring ahead. He kept hearing the sadness and disappointment in Emma's voice. Suddenly he realized why Emma had sounded so let down. He had completely forgotten that tonight was what Emma called their anniversary.

Alan shrugged. Celebrate it another night if she was so stuck on it. It was a silly thing anyway, celebrating the day that they had made the decision to get married. That evening they had made love for the first time and they had pledged their love and loyalty to each other and to stay together forever. It had all been very emotional. It had been Emma's idea to remember that day, now 25 years ago, with a little celebration and to make love like the first time. Alan sighed. Torn between going home to Emma where he belonged or going to this incredible woman who had so fatally ensnared him, exciting him sexually like he had never experienced before. However, it was not the first time that he had felt misgivings about her. For some weeks he had begun to feel guilty about doing this to Emma. He was also very aware that he had been neglecting her. But Emma never complained. She had never questioned where the meetings were held or why in the evening. She had also never asked why he had stopped making love, apart from the occasions when he felt it more or less his duty so as not to completely ignore her.

Alan's hand went to the telephone. He should phone Emma and tell her that he had changed his mind. But, as he picked up the phone, he punched in Saskia's number.

"Yes?" The female voice was soft and throaty. "Saskia, its Alan. I'll be there in about 20 minutes." "OK Alan." A slight pause and then: "Alan!" "Yes."

"I'm ready for you."

CHAPTER 2

They were different and not only in their outward appearance.

Ingrid, a widow, was a small, sporty looking woman in her mid-sixties. During her married life she had played tennis and golf, gone to many social functions and, with her millionaire husband, had often travelled overseas. While her husband was involved in business meetings there, Ingrid visited Art Galleries and attended the opera and ballet, only occasionally accompanied by her husband. Although she no longer went to parties on a regular basis; Ingrid still played her sports and bridge and went to the gym a couple of times a week. She also still went to the opera and ballet with friends from her previous life in Mosman.

Alice, a stoutly built woman in her early sixties was a spinster who, after several failed engagements, had given up on romance and stayed single, resenting others who had found a partner and enjoyed life together.

Several months after moving into her apartment Ingrid discovered that there was another single woman living in the building on the floor above her about her age. Thinking that it would be nice to have a companion to go to the movies with or even an occasional cup of coffee, Ingrid called on her one day.

Alice was polite but reserved, suspicious of Ingrid's motives. However, she invited Ingrid in, took her through to the kitchen and, after some small talk, offered her a cup of tea.

Ingrid, a coffee drinker since her teens who relied on her caffeine fix to get her through the morning, graciously accepted. However, she made a mental note to give Alice a good strong cup of coffee if she ever came to visit.

"Here you are," Alice said as she handed Ingrid her tea. "I never drink coffee. I think it's a drug and the people in our church think so too. You know, I've been told that once you get addicted to it, it ruins your life." She resumed her seat, took a sip of her tea before adding: "I don't trust people who drink coffee."

I won't tell her yet that I'm a drug addict, Ingrid thought, ignoring Alice's last remark. But, if our friendship ever gets off the ground, I will.

"Nice cup of tea, Ingrid said while wishing for a good strong cup of coffee. "So what sort of movies do you usually go to?" Ingrid asked. "Or don't you have a preference."

"I don't like movies with violence. Otherwise I don't mind."

"Well, it would be nice if we could go together if there's something we both want to see. What do you think" It's not much fun going alone all the time."

"That's right," Alice agreed, "and we could discuss it afterwards, don't you think?"

"Yes," Ingrid replied, "that's an interesting thing to do."

"Ingrid, do you go to church?"

Ingrid raised her eyebrows, a bit taken aback at the unexpected question. She shook her head. "No, she said, "never went. I wasn't brought up like that. Nobody in my family ever went to church, neither did my late husband's family."

"Oh well," Alice replied, clearly disappointed. "I suppose there are people like that. But one day you might like to come with me. It's very uplifting and you meet nice people. Of course you have to believe in it."

"Of course, Ingrid answered: "I'm sure that's at the crux of the matter. I'll think about it, Alice. Anyway I must be going. Thanks for the chat and the lovely cup of tea. Now you have to come to my place soon and we'll have a look at what movies are on."

On closing the door Alice went to the kitchen to clean up. She was slightly in awe of Ingrid's obvious wealth, judged by the jewellery she wore on her fingers, wrists and neck, while, at the same time, flattered that this well dressed, sophisticated woman had sorted her out as a companion. Alice was disappointed, however, that Ingrid was not a churchgoer but for the moment she did not want to push that – maybe later when she got to know her better.

Back in her apartment Ingrid made herself a strong cup of coffee. She took it into the lounge room and sat down in a comfortable chair. As she sipped her coffee Ingrid puzzled over Alice. She had noticed that not only was the apartment sparsely furnished but everything looked rather cheap. Surely someone who could afford one of these apartments would have classier furniture. The kitchen was also very bare and, to Ingrid's horror, a plastic tablecloth had covered the wooden table. And the way she was dressed! Ingrid shook her head in disbelief, even though she had come unannounced.

But that was no excuse. Ingrid was always dressed to receive anyone at any time. She recalled that Alice's clothes had been clean but rather worn and faded. Her slacks and blouse had obviously come from K-Mart or some other discount store or even – no, no! Ingrid shook her head at the thought. You're a snob, Ingrid, she admonished herself but nodded in confirmation. Well, all I hope is she dresses better if we go out together.

Ingrid shrugged as she walked to the kitchen and put her cup and saucer in the dishwasher, collected her handbag and went out.

After a hesitant start Ingrid and Alice had struck a friendship of sorts. Besides going to the movies, they met regularly for morning or afternoon tea and occasionally for lunch. Apart from being very different in outlook and both having very strong convictions they got on reasonably well. Ingrid had sorted out her coffee issue on their second meeting, telling Alice that if this friendship was to get off the ground she had better get used to the fact that Ingrid was a 'coffee addict.' Alice had smiled disarmingly, having smelled the aroma of brewed coffee on her arrival. "I really didn't mean to be so adamant about it but I've convinced myself it's bad for me. I don't want to drink it and I try to convince everybody that it's bad for them. Stupid really. Sorry Ingrid."

"It's alright," Ingrid said, "let's take it from here and – she smiled, "I do have tea so I can make you a nice cup." *En passant* noticing that Alice wore very much the same outfit as at their first meeting but this time she had added a necklace and a watch which could have come from a two dollar shop. Ingrid shrugged, so what – but it still puzzled her. One day, she promised herself, she'd ask. She just had to know.

Several weeks after their first meeting Ingrid phoned Alice, suggesting they have afternoon tea together. "You can come here or we can go to the coffee shop downstairs. I've got something very important to tell you about my neighbour and I don't want to tell you over the phone" Ingrid added, cutting off any questions.

"OK. Let's go to the coffee shop."

"Fine. I'll see you there in about 10 minutes."

After they had arrived, Ingrid began her news, having ignored Alice's querying looks until then.

"Yesterday I was about to go out to do some shopping when I saw this elegantly dressed young woman coming out of Saskia's apartment. You know that's the woman on my floor. It looked as if she had already said her goodbye's and was leaving but then she hesitated and turned around. I didn't want to disturb them but I was curious so I stayed inside and didn't quite close my front door. I heard this woman say: "Darling, I do understand that you now want to select your own clients but he doesn't want anyone else, only you. We don't want to lose him. He's very generous and he brings a lot of custom. It's only two nights please! Just this once?" She was really pleading.

"I saw Saskia look at her for a moment then she said with a little smile, "Alright, but this is the last time, Annette, promise! I don't want to spoil my chances."

"I promise and thank you, thank you Saskia. Bye for now."

"Well, it didn't take me long to realise what that was all about. This could only mean one thing. The woman is a prostitute, a call girl. I am sharing this building, my home with a prostitute, a whore" Ingrid added, her voice, slightly raised, trembled with anger and emotion.

Alice frowned, a bit taken aback at Ingrid's outburst. After a short silence and having got herself under control Ingrid said: "It gave me quite a shock. I thought I'd wait till I tell Alice. I'm sure she won't like it either."

"Indeed I don't, Alice said forcefully, "I think it's disgusting and it's going to give the building a bad name with all these dirty men coming and going." Alice shook her head in disbelief. "Who would have thought it, such a nice lady. You can't trust anyone these days, now can you?" she added, taking a bite out of a scone which resulted in cream and jam lodging on her upper lip.

Observing Alice, Ingrid again wondered how this obviously working-class woman had been able to afford buying an apartment in this building.

"Oh, I don't think that's happening so much," Ingrid said, for a moment taking her gaze away from Alice, not wanting her to see her eyes misting over. It was still painful even after all those years. Looking in her bag for a tissue Ingrid added, dabbing her eyes: "No, I think she is rather high class. Escort service I think they call it. I don't think they go out with every Tom, Dick and Harry. No, they pick their clients, steal their money and then dump them, destroying them" Ingrid added bitterly, making Alice look at her briefly, wondering.

"Alright then, so she is not one of those girls standing on street corners, but as far as I am concerned they're all the same and I, er – we don't want her type in the building," Alice said aggressively. "Prostitution is evil. In my church we are taught that your body is the temple of God and selling this temple for money is the Devil's work to discredit him."

Alice looked defiantly at Ingrid, ready to defend her belief, but Ingrid avoided eye contact, busily spreading jam and cream on her second scone. "You wonder if the estate agent knew what she did for a living" Ingrid said, as she deftly popped a piece of scone in her mouth.

Alice shrugged. "He probably didn't worry about it. He's only interested in selling. She probably gave him one of her favours," she added contemptuously. "I'm sure she's good at that!" she said, pulling a face to show her disgust. "Men, they're all the same!

"Show them a bit of naked flesh and they go weak at the knees."

It had taken Ingrid almost a year to find an apartment that not only would match her wealthy widow's status but also had the convenience of being close to shops, restaurants and theatres. Now this woman, this prostitute, was living in the same apartment block, and, of all places, right next door to her. In time, of course, it would lower the tone of the building. Ingrid now kept a close watch on her comings and goings.

A few weeks later as Ingrid and Alice had morning tea together Ingrid said, "Remember I told you about that fellow who was coming around to see her, you know the businessman? Well, it's been going on for some time but of course up to now I haven't taken much notice. I think he's a boyfriend. He's very regular but what puzzles me is that they never go out. He never takes her anywhere."

"A boyfriend, Alice exclaimed, "A boyfriend? Come on now," she continued as she lowered her voice and quickly looked around to see if anyone had heard. "People like that don't have boyfriends. I thought they were called pimps."

"Well, anyway, he's there often enough and I haven't seen any other men."

"Amazing," Alice said, adding rather sarcastically, "and what does he look like this er-boyfriend?"

Ingrid shrugged. "Well, I'd say he's around the fifties, tallish, good looking, always well dressed, you know, suit and tie. I'm sure he's a businessman."

"Huh," Alice sneered, pulling a face, "let's wait and see what happens. It'll be a nine-day wonder, you'll see. These people don't have steady relationships. They're used to too much variety. Anyway, whatever, businessman or no businessman, she's got to go!" Alice added firmly.

SASKIA'S DIARY

I have now stopped seeing clients. Alan and I have such a good relationship that I think we should be living together. I have been thinking about that for some time but somehow never got around to suggesting it.

But tonight I will.

Marrying him is probably setting my sights too high, at least for the moment. But I love him so much. I so hope that Alan never finds out what I did for a living because I don't know how he will take that. However, if his love for me is strong enough I hope, or should I say, I'm sure it will not matter.

CHAPTER 3

The view from the balcony was magnificent. It looked out over Whale Beach and the wide expanse of the Tasman Sea beyond. The waves, lazily rolling towards the shore, glistened in the rapidly rising sun.

After getting out of bed Alan would, habitually, go out onto the balcony, suck his lungs full of crisp clean morning air and marvel at the scenery. This morning, however, as he leaned on the balcony railing, Alan Henderson stared morosely ahead, his mind on the previous night.

"It's late, my darling. I must go. I hate leaving you but I have to go." Alan began to sit up but Saskia pulled him down towards her.

In a throaty whisper she asked, "Do you like me, Alan, really like me?"

Hugging and kissing her, Alan said, "Of course, my darling, I like you. I love you."

"I love you too very much and I've been wondering why we're living like this. Instead of coming here for a few hours once or twice a week; it would be nicer and easier if you moved in with me. I love you, Alan, and I'm always looking forward to your next visit.

Alan had had a fitful night worrying about it. But now in the cold light of day he was more angry than worried. He should have known something was amiss. Lately Saskia had not been herself. The last few times he had been with her he had found her looking at him as if she wanted to say something but she seemed unsure how to say it. Well, she had said it now.

There had been a time when Alan too had toyed with the same idea in the early days of their romance. Life would be different, but how different and did he really want this to happen? Besides, he knew nothing about her and as he thought it through he decided it wasn't worth all the upheaval. Moving in with her! Alan shook his head. For God's sake, that was not what this was about.

But I've been stupid, he thought. I shouldn't have gone so often. Naturally, she had begun to think that there was more to their relationship. Alan frowned and shook his head. If only he could remember what had happened. Had he answered her or had he just walked out? He couldn't remember getting dressed and leaving her apartment. But would Saskia leave it at that? A sudden tightening of his chest gripped him. She might try to contact him at work or, worse still, at home. She could very well turn up on his doorstep and this petrified him. There had been times when he had considered not going back to her but, like an addict reaching for a cigarette, Alan would pick up the phone and tell her that he was on his way.

At least now, and Alan was relieved about this, his dilemma had been resolved. There was no future in their relationship and there never had been. Alan had no intention of leaving Emma – his Emma, no vices, no demands, just a loving wife who was always there when he needed her.

"Penny for your thoughts?"

Absorbed in his reflections, Alan jumped at the unexpected voice at his side. "Christ, Emma, don't do that," he said, his voice raised in irritation.

"Sorry, darling if I startled you," Emma put an arm around his waist and snuggled up to him.

"It's alright," Alan said gruffly, annoyed at his reaction. He felt her pressed against him but he did not respond. Last night had upset him too much. Besides his lovemaking with Saskia was still too fresh in his mind for him to play the loving husband to the woman he had been betraying for so long.

"Were you late last night? I didn't hear you come in."

"No, not that late, no later than usual," Alan lied easily, trying to hide his anxiety.

"I was tired," pensively Emma looked out to sea. "I don't know why. It's not that I lead such a hectic life. I just don't seem to have any energy."

She had wanted to tell him for some time that she had been having pains in her abdomen and she had finally gone to the doctor, but she held back. Looking at her husband she noticed the muscles working in his handsome face and the dark angry look as he stared out over the ocean. It did not encourage her to talk about her problems.

She doubted whether he had heard what she had just told him. Emma could not understand why he had become like this – moody and sometimes downright rude. Was it her or was there someone else and he wanted to be rid of her? Emma was afraid to ask in case he used the opportunity to tell her that he was leaving her.

Alan did not answer or look at her.

Hurt by his indifference, Emma withdrew her arm and said casually, "Well, let's have breakfast."

CHAPTER 4

The weather was warm and humid. Low dark clouds hung overhead promising rain. Inside, the air was muggy and oppressive. Occasional wafts of cool air from the Tasman Sea drifted onto the verandah where Emma, preferring this to the air-conditioning inside, had stretched out on a deckchair, cool drink by her side and her book unopened in her lap. Her mood matched the weather as she stared sombrely ahead. No matter what she was doing, or planned to do, her thoughts would inevitably turn to Alan, his behaviour and her now strongly firming belief that there was another woman involved. Perhaps there had been another woman all along and those late-night meetings were with her.

It would also explain why he had hardly come near her in the last four to five months.

Not having been well for some time with a nagging pain in her stomach Emma had only been too pleased that Alan had not made many demands on her. When he did she had given in only to please him. She had always put his lack of interest making love down to stress and the long hours at work. Trusting Alan implicitly Emma always accepted his explanations, even if there had been occasions when she had wondered about a whiff of unfamiliar perfume. But there were women on the board and Emma hadn't given it another thought.

But what should she do if there was another woman? Tell him to pack his bags? Put up with it? Ask for a divorce? Or should she leave? A sudden stab of pain interrupted her thoughts making her grimace and she pushed against her stomach with her fists. After a little while the pain eased somewhat and she went inside to take another painkiller.

For several weeks Emma had been able to control the pain with medication but over the last few weeks the pain had become intense and more difficult to control and she had finally gone to her doctor. While not exactly reading the riot act, the doctor had sternly admonished Emma for taking so long to come to see her. Now she was awaiting the test results.

Emma sighed. She was doing a lot of sighing lately. Taking a sip from her drink, she picked up her book, determined to put it out of her mind until she heard from the doctor. As she gazed at the print she reasoned that it probably was nothing serious, maybe just a nasty ulcer – nothing to worry about really.

Nevertheless, Emma was worried, no matter how brave a face she put on. It was not so much what the doctor had said as what she hadn't said. Maybe she should talk to Marjorie. She had to confide in someone, otherwise she'd go mad. There were times when she couldn't think straight anymore. A sudden gust of wind and a few drops of rain made up Emma's mind. After folding up the deck chair and leaving it against the house she went to the wall phone in the kitchen and pushed in Marjorie's number.

"Hi, Marj, it's Emma. How are you?" Emma said trying to sound cheerful but not succeeding.

"Emma, you alright?" Marjorie said, alarmed at Emma's tone of voice.

"Yes, I'm alright, just a bit down, that's all. Do you mind if I come around?"

"No, of course not and you've phoned at the right time. I've just made a cake. Now, don't laugh, I did! Well, see you soon. Bye for now."

Twenty minutes later Emma was sitting at Marjorie's table in the family room having a cup of coffee and sampling the cake. Living less than fifteen minutes' walk away from each other, Emma had walked, feeling rather good for having done that. The rain that had been threatening earlier had cleared.

"The cake is beautiful," Emma said, "No really, I mean it."

"I'll give you the recipe if you like," Marjorie said, pleased with the compliment. "It's an old recipe of my Aunt's. Apparently, she was the cake maker in the family."

Looking at Emma a bit more closely, she added, "It looks like you can do with a bit of extra on you. You've lost a lot of weight, my girl. Are you on a diet or something? Tell me about it, I seem to be packing it on." Marjorie patted her sides, "come to think of it I thought you were a bit on the thin side when I saw you last and that's about three weeks ago, from memory."

"No, I'm not on a diet, just feeling a bit off lately."

"What's Alan think about it? You know, about you losing weight and all that. I mean, if I notice it?"

For a few moments Emma looked at Marjorie then, covering her face with her hands she began to cry.

"Hey, hey, what's the matter? What's going on, Emma?" Marjorie said anxiously, frowning as she leaned forward to look searchingly at her friend.

Taking a tissue out of her handbag Emma wiped her eyes and regained her composure.

"I'm sorry, Marj. I didn't mean to. It's just that –" Emma paused, then she said more firmly, "I think there is another woman."

Raising her eyebrows, Marjorie said in an incredulous tone, "Another woman Alan! Another woman!" Marjorie shook her head and pursed her mouth. "I don't believe it! My God, he worships the ground you walk on. He won't kiss me on the lips or give me a sexy cuddle because he's afraid you'll get upset. Him! Another woman! Ha!"

"Well" Emma hesitated, somewhat taken aback by Marjorie's extraordinary reaction, "He hardly kisses me. He hasn't put his arms around me for a long time. You know, a real hug that makes you feel good and wanted. I always thought it was pressure at work. There have been some difficulties and he has been under a lot of strain. He's always at the office or at a meeting, sometimes till late at night."

"Have you talked to him about it?" Emma shook her head.

"Well that's what I would do," Marjorie said firmly. "Confront him, ask him what is going on?"

Emma shrugged. "I really don't know what to make of it, Marj, maybe it's me."

"Nonsense," Marjorie said emphatically. "It's not you. It's him."

"I'm not sure," Emma said tearily, as she plucked at the tissue. "He hardly makes love to me and the few times it did happen it was as if he felt obliged to do it. There was no love, no feeling, no kiss, no hug, nothing! He didn't make love to me Marj. It was just sex. I felt like a prostitute. Maybe he would have shown more feeling with one of them? I wanted him so much but it was all over before it started. That night something died in me, Marj, and I can't bring it back to life, not yet anyway. And, by the way he behaves now, it won't come back. I show affection but it is all met with a certain indifference. Sometimes he is downright rude and distant."

Marjorie shook her head. "I don't understand. I really don't. I mean it is so totally out of character. He was always so proper, always wanting to do the right thing. Anyway," Marjorie continued, resolutely, "you must talk to him. You have to find out what's going on, for your own piece of mind. Otherwise it will drive you crazy. Put it to him straight. Don't beat around the bush! Say something like, are you screwing someone else? Am I not good enough anymore? That'll make him sit up, the bastard. You can't just leave it and hope that it will sort itself out, because from what you have just told me, it won't."

"OK, and then what?" Emma countered. "What if he says yes, that he's screwing another woman?"

"Well, then, at least you know where you stand. But somehow I get the feeling you really don't want to know. Am I right?"

Emma didn't answer immediately. Fidgeting with the tissue she looked away. Then turning back to Marjorie, she said, "I don't know, Marj. Maybe you're right. All I know is that I think about it all the time, trying to work out where I went wrong. But I can't think of anything, sexually or otherwise. But maybe there is and he is looking elsewhere. He's hardly ever home. He spends more time with his secretary than with me."

"Now, Emma, you mustn't read anything into that. People at work spend their days with their colleagues, Bill too. He is away all day in his office with his secretary. But I can't get upset about that. I'd be a nervous wreck!"

"Yes, but can't you see what I'm thinking? I'm getting paranoid about it. I picture them in the office having sex. Yes, alright, it may not be her but someone is getting it because I'm not and I don't think he's turned celebate! It's not so much the sex but I miss the warmth of his arms around me, his gentle kisses. I'm ignored, Marj. He has become estranged from me and I don't know how to handle it. In spite of this, I find I still love him. I don't want to lose him but I think I have."

Looking despairingly at her friend, Emma's eyes filled with tears. "I'm sorry, Marj, I didn't want to tell you but you're my closest friend and I needed to talk. I may have been able to cope, but after my visit to the doctor I couldn't take anymore."

"Doctor? Marjorie queried. "Why did you have to go to the doctor? Did he beat you up?"

"No, no, it's nothing like that," Emma said hastily and looking away from Marjorie she added, "I'm sorry, it's nothing. I had to go to the doctor, that's all."

"Sorry no, that's not all" Marjorie said sternly trying to make eye contact.

"There's more to it than that," Marjorie said, hating herself for being so bossy but there was something else worrying Emma, apart from Alan's alleged infidelity, and as her friend, she wanted to get to the bottom of it. She knew Emma too well. Not only had Emma been uncharacteristically nervous, but several times Marjorie had observed her staring out the window, her mind on something else.

"W—e—ll," Emma began after a short silence, "I've been having pains in my stomach. It would settle down for a while and I thought it had something to do with Alan's behaviour. You know, like tying your stomach in a knot, but it got worse."

"What did the doctor say?"

Emma shrugged and looked away. "Nothing, she didn't commit herself. I've had some tests and have to wait for the results."

"How long have you had the pain?"

Emma gave Marjorie a quick glance and shrugged. "4 or 5 weeks. I can't remember exactly. Anyway—"

"4 or 5 weeks!" Marjorie interrupted, raising her voice. "4 or 5 weeks! What's the matter with you to let it go on for so long? I don't understand, I really don't, Emma."

Looking helplessly at Marjorie and fighting back tears, Emma said, "Yes, I have been stupid. Thinking about it now, I can't understand it myself. It probably was a combination of things. I felt that I had lost Alan but I didn't feel mentally strong enough to challenge him and also I wondered what he would do, if I did. So I took the easy way out and said nothing."

"Oh, you poor darling, why didn't you talk to me?" Marjorie said, "It needn't have gone as far as this."

"I don't know, Marj. I really don't, maybe I was ashamed to admit that I had lost Alan, that our married life was non-existent. I became almost immune to his indifference and put on the pretence of being the loving wife when we were out together." After a short pause Emma added, "So there it is, Marj. It is a terrible mess and I don't know what to do about it."

"Have you told Alan that you've been to the doctor? Have you told him anything?"

Emma shook her head.

"I think you should! He must know, Emma."

"Yes, I should have told him," Emma said resignedly, "but I'm afraid that he will shrug it off or tell me to stop complaining. That's been his attitude for a while now. I really don't know what's got into him."

"Well, you'll have to find out," Marjorie said firmly. "Now don't be too proud to talk to me. We've known each other since we were in kindergarten and you're more like a sister to me. I'm sorry if I sound bossy but I want you to promise that you'll come and talk to me, if there is anything worrying you. Promise?"

Tearfully Emma whispered, "I promise."

CHAPTER 5

Alan Henderson was at his desk in his study going over his estimates for the last quarter of his year's growth. He couldn't afford a slip-up. It had to be water-tight. The board meeting was this morning at 11.00 a.m. But, while looking at the figures his thoughts kept slipping back to the morning on the balcony. He grimaced as he recalled glancing at Emma and noticing for the first time how thin she was. He wondered now, as he had then, how long she had been like that. Indeed, how long had it been since he had looked at Emma and really seen her. Feeling the guilt of neglect gnawing at him, Alan leant back. What has been happening he asked himself. Had his obsession with Saskia, because that was what it had ever been, made him blind to the needs of Emma? He felt as if he had been living in a vacuum and had suddenly been catapulted back to reality.

Alan sighed and looked at his watch. Twenty to nine. Then it registered and he looked again. "20 to bloody nine." He almost shouted the time. He had been sitting here for far too long. He should have been well and truly on his way. He gathered his papers and put them in his briefcase, pushed pen and calculator into a corner of his desk and just as he got up the phone rang. He waited to see if Emma was going to answer it but after several rings he realized that she obviously wasn't near a phone and he picked it up.

"Yes," Alan said, rather abrupt, annoyed with himself for having answered it. "Mr Henderson?"

"Yes, speaking."

"It's Dr Mansell, Mr Henderson, I – "

"Oh, excuse me doctor," Alan interrupted impatiently, "I don't know what this is about but you obviously want to speak to my wife. I'll get her for you. I was just on my way out."

"Well actually Mr Henderson, I am afraid it concerns both of you. I would like you both to come to my surgery this morning. It is about your wife. I have made the appointment for 10 o'clock. Maybe you will be good enough to tell Mrs Henderson?"

Alan looked at his watch and shook his head obstinately, thinking, out of the question. This morning's meeting was crucial to the next quarter of business. He just had to be there. "Look, doctor" he began persuasively, "I have to---"

"Mr Henderson, I am very sorry but I feel that it is important that you both come to see me. I wouldn't have made this appointment on your behalf if it wasn't."

Alan, his jaw set firmly, didn't answer. He just had to be at that meeting. There was too much at stake. Any other bloody time would have been OK. And why was this so bloody important that he had to be there as well.

While he was still thinking of refusing to go, Dr Mansell said, "Mr Henderson?" questioning but leaving no doubt as to what she expected him to say.

Alan sighed, hesitated briefly and then gave in.

"Yes, yes," he said impatiently, curtly. "I'll be there." "Thank you Mr Henderson."

Frowning, Alan put the phone back on its station. He stood for a moment, wondering what it was about. He'd almost asked but he would have made a proper fool of himself for not knowing. But surely, Alan frowned, Emma would have told me if there was something seriously wrong with her. But she hadn't said anything, so it really couldn't be anything serious. What if he hadn't picked up the phone or, if he had been on his way as he had intended to be? Well, he bloody well hadn't left and he bloody well had picked up the bloody phone. He sat down again. Better get onto Liza, he muttered and punched in the numbers of his direct line into his office.

"Liza, Alan here. Yes, yes, good morning" he answered curtly, still upset at the turn of events. Look, something has come up at home," Alan continued, softening his voice. "I can't be at the meeting, so I'll fax you my notes and comments and I'm afraid you'll have to deliver them. I'm sorry about this, but at least you are familiar with this. Any questions and feedback I'll attend to as soon as possible. And please offer them my apologies."

"Yes, Mr Henderson, of course I'll look after it."

"I know you will. I'll see you later. Bye for now."

A smile now crossed his face. Good girl Liza. She had been with him now nearly three years and she was the best and most efficient secretary he had ever had. She may call him Alan in the sanctuary of their offices, but outside or on the phone it was always Mr Henderson.

Alan pushed his chair away from his desk, muttering 'this had better be bloody important,' and went looking for Emma, finding her in the laundry.

"Emma, I just had —"

"Alan," Emma interrupted, surprised to see him, "I thought you'd already gone."

Ignoring this and still put out about giving in to the doctor, Alan said rather gruffly, "I had a phone call from Dr Mansell. She wants us both to come to the surgery this morning. Now, I want to bloody well know what this is all about. I haven't got the bloody --- hey, what's the matter, what's going on?" Alan demanded, when Emma visually paled and held onto the wash tub.

"Are you sick? Why didn't you tell me you've been to see a doctor!"

Regaining her composure, Emma looked at Alan, her face taut in sudden anger.

"Tell you?" she said. "Tell you?" she repeated, raising her voice. "You have the gall to ask me why I didn't tell you? How long has it been since you have taken any interest in me?" Emma was shouting now, her voice unleashing the pent up suffering and humiliation.

"Yes, when was the last time you asked how I felt? When was the last time you held me in your arms and made love to me? Can you remember? I can. I can very well remember the last time you fucked me. You've used this place as a boarding house and me as the maid. And finally, in answer to your question, I don't know what she wants to tell us, so I suppose we had better go? Or maybe you are having one of your exciting meetings and you can't make it? But don't worry Alan, I can go by myself. I've been doing a lot of things by myself for a long time.

Emma stopped abruptly, surprised and taken aback by her outburst. She had not wanted to say all this. She had not wanted to say anything at all. But the words had come spontaneously, triggered by Alan's affronting demand to know why she hadn't told him she'd been to see a doctor.

"The appointment is at 10 o'clock," Alan said tensely, "and I'm coming."

Staring angrily at Emma he opened his mouth to say something but instead turned and strode away.

Emma, watched him walked away. It felt as if just then he had walked out of her life. Tears welled up in her eyes. There had been no sympathy, no concern for her wellbeing. Only anger. For a moment Emma remained very still, saddened and distressed at what had just happened. Then, taking a deep breath, her face set determinately, she closed the lid to the washing machine and after turning on the power, went upstairs to get dressed.

By the time Alan got back to his study his anger had subsided. He sat down at his desk and leaning back stared morosely ahead of him. Emma's words had hit home, harder and deeper than he could have imagined. And now, and maybe for the first time he really understood and realized what he had subjected Emma to.

Looking back at it, it seemed inconceivable that he had done this to her. He loved her, he always had. Those other women meant nothing to him. It had nothing to do with his love for Emma. It was just – Alan shrugged. He hadn't even meant it to go this far but somehow it got away from him. It had been there for the taking and he had taken it. It had boosted his ego no end that he, at the age of 50 could woo and seduce women, some more than half his age. Soon it became a challenge, then a need to prove himself. Then he met Saskia. He hadn't looked at another woman since. It had been the start of a relationship he hadn't really wanted but didn't know how to end. Partly because deep down he didn't want to end it. But what had happened that night had scared and unsettled him. It had suddenly made him realise how far this had gone and how deep his involvement with her was. He hadn't heard from Saskia since that night and he hoped he never would.

He looked at his watch – 9.30 – they had better go.

CHAPTER 6

Even though looking straight at the doctor, Alan's mind was on the meeting, wondering if Liza could handle it.

"I should have been there," he thought, "there was too much at stake."

He pictured them sitting at the boardroom table picking holes in his estimates and Liza trying to defend them. Charlie for sure would have a go, happy he was not there. Keith too would be putting the screws on Liza. Nodding to himself he muttered inaudibly. 'Yes, I should have been there instead of wasting my –'

Suddenly Alan became aware of the silence hanging heavily in the room. Up to now the doctor's voice had been mere background to his thoughts. But the silence propelled him back in the surgery. He became aware now too of the doctor looking at him.

Dr Mansell had never met Alan Henderson and her first impression of him had been one of arrogance, a patronizing arrogance. When Emma introduced Alan to her doctor, Alan had let her know that he had taken time out from his busy schedule to be here and that she should be grateful for his presence.

"Er – sorry doctor, I'm afraid I didn't hear what you said."

Dr Mansell nodded and said: "I've told Emma that the pain in her stomach was caused by what we think is a rather advanced tumour and of course…"

"What? A tumour? Cancer?" Alan flared up interrupting the doctor, "What are you talking about?"

"I didn't say it is cancer," Dr Mansell answered quietly. "We don't know until we do a biopsy. It may be just a non-malignant growth."

Dr Mansell stopped. The tests had shown the tumour might be malignant. Her dilemma, and she had agonized over this had been, should she give false hope or tell them the chance of recovery was 50/50. She felt terrible and very sorry for Emma whom she had known for a long time. Her professional detachment honed to perfection through ssion never completely cancelled out compassion.

Looking angrily at the doctor and raising his voice, Alan said, "You don't know? How come you don't know? How long has this been going on for and why haven't you done anything about it until now?"

Turning to Emma he began, "Darling ---," but stopped when he saw her face and a chill ran down his spine.

'She knows,' flashed through his mind when he saw the look of anguish on her marble, white face. 'She knew, she knew all along she had cancer and she never told me.'

Suddenly the surgery and everything in it began to float and spin. Instinctively Alan gripped the arms of the chair and gulped air. He heard a voice but it came from so far away he couldn't hear what was being said. Just as he thought he was going to faint, he recovered. As he opened his eyes he saw the doctor standing next to him looking concerned. He nodded to say he was alright and, although feeling shaky, got up and went to Emma. Full of love and compassion, his eyes brimming with tears he wanted to put his arms around her to comfort her, to be her strength in this terrible ordeal. That's what he meant to do.

Instead he sagged to his knees, buried his head in Emma's lap and broke down. He cried, his body jerking with the sobs that came from deep within him because of the guilt and remorse of what he had done to her. Stroking his head, comforting him, Emma now too began to weep.

Alan finally got up. Studiously avoiding looking at Emma, he went back to his chair and, perplexed, sat down. He couldn't believe what he had just found out about himself. He had always seen himself, and he believed other people saw him, as a sound, well balanced man with a strong personality who would not fall apart when tragedy struck, even when feeling guilty and remorseful. He was shocked to find that it was not quite like that and it had profoundly unsettled him. He had not only failed Emma, but more importantly he had failed himself. But what had really surprised him, and this even more than his apparent lack of it, was the strength and calm with which Emma had accepted the doctor's prognosis. It was a quality in her he had not known she possessed. She had been the strength for both of them. He winced when he thought of her crying when she stroked his head. Obviously she had felt sorry for him.

They waited, wordlessly, holding hands until the doctor, who had discreetly left the room, returned.

Immediately after coming home from the doctor, Alan phoned his secretary, Liza, "Yes thank you, I'm fine" he said, somewhat impatiently. "I won't be coming in for a couple of days. Something has come up and I will tell you about it later. If you need me for anything, anything at all, give me a ring, email or fax me. And – er – can you fax me the minutes of the board meeting and add your own impressions of how it went. Thank you Liza. I'll be in touch, bye."

Two days later Emma went into hospital. Every afternoon Alan went to see her. Often he would just sit there, holding her hand, his whole being brimming over with love, while being tormented with guilt.

Coming home late afternoon on the day of Emma's operation Alan suddenly felt the full impact of loneliness as he, deeply depressed wandered through the rooms, the stillness accentuated by the sound of shoes on the parquetry floors, emphasizing the emptiness of his existence without Emma. But this was what he had subjected Emma to. He imagined Emma wandering through the house, alone and lonely while he ….'I'm sorry Emma' he sobbed, 'I'm so very sorry. I love you so.'

He sank in one of the comfortable lounge chairs in the living room and every time he closed his eyes he saw Emma lying in her hospital bed, very pale and her eyes closed. But every now and then Emma would open her eyes, look at him and smile. It was the smile that disturbed him most. Alan remained in the chair because going to sleep in his bed right now would remind him of the many nights Emma had gone to bed with him not being there.

Alan woke when the first light came through the windows. Stiffly he got up, out of the chair and went upstairs to have a shower. This usually made him feel good and set him up for the day. This morning it had no effect. He made himself a cup of coffee and took it onto the balcony, still feeling totally miserable. He kept seeing Emma, pale and thin, smiling at him. The smile that said, "I love you."

SASKIA'S DIARY

I have not been able to write in my diary for almost a week now. I just couldn't sit down and write about my feelings. I am devastated, my whole world has collapsed.

The man I love so much has not been in touch with me at all after leaving me that fateful night. But I'm writing in my diary now because I have to put down some of my feelings and thoughts, otherwise I'll go mad. I've never been so hurt in my whole life. When I asked if he would consider moving in with me which I thought to be a logical follow on what was between us, he got out of bed and left without a word, without even looking at me.

I haven't seen or heard from him since. I don't understand. Unless, and I have had my suspicions, he is married and he hasn't got the guts to tell his wife he is in love with another woman. I thought we had a relationship, a relationship we could build on and develop if we were together, if we did other things apart from making love.

I thought I knew men!! To say that I've been naïve is an understatement!

I don't know what to do now? I love him. I really love him. Maybe if I write to him, tell him how and what I feel, tell him about my love for him, he may change his mind and come back to me For him to be so loving and kind to me, surely means he really does not love his wife.

After a few days of agonizing over it I have now written him a letter. I looked up to see where he lives to make sure he gets it, I am going to deliver it myself. I watched him taking it out of the box and seeing him I nearly ran out to him but something stopped me doing it. I have been thinking about that but I can't explain it. But I'm sure now he's married. No wonder he never ever stayed the night!

CHAPTER 7

Much had happened since the evening Alan had walked out on Saskia and although thinking of her, he hoped he would never see or hear from her again. Saskia asking him to move in with her had been a wake-up call. It had told him, rather brutally, how deep this had gone and obviously what it meant for her. All it had been for Alan had been an obsession of conquering women for sex, trying to prove himself. But Emma's sickness and hospitalisation had brought home to him how much he loved her and how stupid this all had been. From now on he would devote all his spare time to Emma, helping her to get better and come home soon. So, when picking up his mail one evening and seeing amongst the white business envelopes, a hand addressed violet coloured small envelope his heart skipped a beat and there was a sinking feeling in his stomach. There could not be any doubt. This could only be from her. He hurried inside and throwing the business letters on the kitchen table he ripped the violet coloured envelope open and read:

My Dearest, Dearest Alan,

I have been waiting for you to call me. I hope you are not sick because if you are I want to come and look after you. I miss you. I miss you terribly. If you are not sick why haven't you come to see me? I cannot bear it not hearing from you. I will phone you if I don't hear from you soon. I miss you. I love you, I miss you.

Forever yours.
Saskia

Not quite believing what he was reading he read the letter again, but it still took a little while before the full meaning of the letter finally sunk in and a bolt of unease went through him. This was not only not good, this was terrible. He had no intention of ever going back to her and he had thought not contacting her would have made this clear.

But what to do now, he thought, sitting down and putting the letter on the table. Ignore this? Or should I write to tell her I have no intention of ever coming to see her again?

It had terribly unsettled him and he sat for a while just staring ahead, occasionally his mind a blank and then coming back to think about what to do about this. In the end he decided to ignore it. It would be for the best to not make contact at all. She should get the message then that he wasn't going back to her. He was finished with her and all his womanizing. He had to look after Emma and make up for the times he had neglected her. And while thinking about that, guilt gnawed at his very being.

Finally, sighing deeply, Alan put the letter back in its envelope and went upstairs to his study. Sitting at his desk he pulled out the bottom left hand drawer and was about to put the letter in when he noticed that there was no stamp. This could only mean one thing. 'Bloody hell,' he mumbled, 'she's hand delivered it. She found out where I live. The bloody woman has been to my house.' Closing the drawer Alan locked it, picked up the phone and ordered a pizza. Going back downstairs he poured himself a scotch and looking at the news on T.V. waited for his pizza to arrive.

CHAPTER 8

"Lovely place," Alice said, looking around, her gaze finally settling on the marina with the yachts bobbing in the water. "I never knew this existed. I just never went to this side of the harbour."

"Yes, it's nice," Ingrid answered, casually twisting the gold bracelets on her left arm. Alice, looking at her thinking 'bloody show off...'

"Yes, it's beautiful. I thought it'd be a nice change from the city. Er – we used to live around here in Cremorne." Ingrid added after a slight pause.

"Oh, did you? To me it looks a pretty expensive area?"

Ingrid didn't notice the slight undertone of envy. "There are lots of lovely places in this area," Ingrid said enthusiastically, "we loved it here."

"Then why did you leave? You obviously belong here amongst the upper crust?" Now Ingrid looked at Alice. This time there was no mistaking the tone.

Alice shrugged. "Never had much to do with people like you" she continued. "I'm just ordinary working class. For most of my life I had to work hard to make ends meet. But then I became a carer for a very rich old lady through the church. We got on well together and when she died she left me enough money to buy the apartment and also live comfortably."

"Well, join the upper crust," Ingrid said, making a joke of it. For a moment it looked as if it wasn't appreciated, then Alice's face softened,

"Sorry Ingrid," she said, "I didn't mean to offend you. Friends again?"

"Of course," Ingrid said light-heartedly, "Anyway to answer your question, when my husband died, I wanted somewhere different. This area reminded me too much of him, of the times we had together here. And I love going to the opera and ballet and living in the city makes going to them a lot easier."

"I went once, to the opera," Alice said, "The old lady loved it too. But I didn't have a clue what was going on. And I have never been to a ballet. The old lady's friends usually took her."

"OK." Ingrid said, "When we have morning tea at my place next I'll play you some opera and ballet music. I'm sure you'd like it."

Alice shrugged: "Possible, I don't go much for this classical stuff."

"Let's wait and see. You might surprise yourself. Anyway I meant to tell you the businessman stopped coming. It's been a couple of weeks now and I haven't seen him."

"He's probably on holidays or on a business trip," Alice said, slicing a piece of her salmon and putting it in her mouth.

"Yes, I thought that too at first," Ingrid said, taking a sip of her wine, "but I've noticed Saskia looking unhappy, depressed even."

"My salmon is so nice," Alice said after some silence, "How is your lamb?"

"Beautiful," Ingrid said. "You know, we are very lucky to be able to enjoy all this; a beautiful day, a beautiful meal, and beautiful company, she added with a cheeky grin.

Alice smiled, "What can I say?" Anyway, let's get back to our problem." Sipping her wine she said "You know what I think, I think the businessman has given her the boot. He probably found out what she is doing on the side because I'm sure she is not retiring. She is too young and too beautiful for that."

"You're probably right but I wish she had taken her business somewhere else," Ingrid said, thinking how the coming of the businessman had affected her. She had begun to visualize and fantasise about what he was obviously coming for and it had brought to the surface a desire Ingrid thought she had buried along with her husband. Indeed for the almost two years she had been a widow, Ingrid had not felt the need or the urge to have a sexual relationship. But Saskia and the businessman had changed that.

"So I think she'll stay," Alice said interrupting Ingrid's thoughts, "the address gives her a certain class."

"Yes, probably so, but I can't stand living next to a whore, and I am not going to move."

"Well, in that case we'll have to start thinking of how to move her, maybe like – on a stretcher, Alice looked serious.

"Alice!!" Ingrid chided, frowning appearing to be shocked, then, looking mischievously, "You mean sort of lifeless."

"Tsk -Tsk," Alice shook her head, "That's a terrible thing to say," she said quasi sternly, then she laughed, "Maybe."

Ingrid became serious, recalling how close she had been to doing something really stupid. She had been watching from her front door, which she often did to look at the businessman, trying to find a way to attract his attention, and dress accordingly that particular evening, as soon as she saw the businessman stepping out of the lift, Ingrid, in a low cut dress, her breasts propped up as high as she could get them and very visible, walked slowly, coquettishly, past him.

So to add insult to injury, the businessman, instead of ignoring her, gave her just one contemptuous glance and turned his back on her. Ingrid, her self-esteem suitably dented and her hate for Saskia increased, went back to her apartment.

Thinking back on this now Ingrid found it hard to believe she had done this. But she had. She had wanted the businessman all to herself and in her bed. And now, every time the businessman came those feelings got stronger than Ingrid would have liked, so she would lie on her bed and pretend he was with her making love. And now she didn't even have to see the businessman. Just looking at Saskia's front door was enough to make her loins ache with the want for him.

'I'm besotted like a stupid little school girl' Ingrid thought. 'Now if I remove the cause…'

"Penny for your thoughts" Alice said, looking closely at Ingrid, "You've been quiet for a while."

"I've been thinking of a way to get rid of the whore and not getting blamed for it," Ingrid said, smiling sweetly.

Appearing to be shocked, Alice shook her head" "Tse - Tse" she said, then, leaving forward she added eagerly "Did you think of something?"

"No, Ingrid shook her head, "But I'm working on it," she added brightly.

"Well, good luck with it. Do you mind if we go now Ingrid. I really have to do some shopping?"

"No, not at all."

"You can let me out here," Alice said when they approached the corner of York and Market Street, "And thanks. I'll be in touch. There is a film being released and I would like to see it. Anyway we'll talk about it. See you later and thanks again."

Alice watched Ingrid drive away with mixed feelings. Did she like her? Alice shrugged involuntarily. In some way she did. But often, like now envy bordering on dislike got the upper hand. She admitted, albeit that she was envious of Ingrid's privileged upbringing and subsequent life in a posh suburb with a wealthy husband. Ingrid, refined and ladylike contrasted with Alice's often coarse and plebeian behaviour. Ingrid who played golf, bridge and tennis. Things Alice had never been able to participate in. She also resented Ingrid's often, and she was sure unintentional patronizing attitude.

Going to the grand opera houses in Europe to see opera and ballet had been part of Ingrid's life and sometimes Ingrid got carried away talking about it, reliving that part of her life she had enjoyed so much. But in doing this, Ingrid was driving the knife of envy and bitterness a bit deeper every time. Alice was well aware that it had been loneliness and the need of a ready companion that had made Ingrid contact her. She had probably thought that people living in these apartments were of the same social standing as she. That Ingrid had stuck with her, Alice reasoned, was because there was nobody else around. It didn't even occur to Alice to think that Ingrid just might be sincere about her friendship with her.

Driving home, Ingrid reflected on how close it had come for her to get involved with the businessman. She found it difficult to understand now because not having seen the man for some time now, her desire to have him in her bed had greatly diminished. And she could understand even less now why at the time she had been so hell-bent in giving up her independence and for what? She thought as she neatly parked her car, for a bit of sex? I must have taken leave of my senses, she mused as she took the lift to the fourth floor.

CHAPTER 9

It was now six days since Saskia's letter and Alan was sure now that ignoring it had been the right thing. It looked like she had got the message. Every day while picking up his newspaper, he had been looking in the mailbox but when she had not made contact Alan had begun to relax and stopped looking.

Happier and less pre-occupied than he had been for some time, Alan walked onto the nature-strip, picked up his newspaper. As he turned around he glanced at the mailbox and the jolt hit him right in the pit of his stomach. There it was, sticking halfway out of the slot. Alan stared at it as if transfixed, then snatched it out, hurried back inside and up to his study. Nervously he slid the top and took out the thin note-sized paper. It was red. The first thing he saw were the flowers in the top right-hand corner, cut out of a magazine and glued in. They were forget-me-nots.

My Darling Alan,

I know you are busy my Darling, but that never stopped you from contacting me. What happened Alan? I miss you so much. Please, please answer me. Why didn't you answer my earlier letter? I know you have it. I love you Alan, I love you very much.

You love me too. You told me this more than once. You are always in my thoughts. Please contact me.

Yours forever Saskia xxxxxx

Alan put the letter on his desk and beginning to feel very uneasy leaned back in his chair, thinking what now? It didn't look like she was going to let him go that easily. He was annoyed with himself for thinking that she would. He had been involved with her, going to her two, occasionally even three times a week. 'O.K. So, I've been stupid.'

For a few moments he sat, staring broodingly ahead of him, angry for not thinking of the consequences, letting his infatuation with the woman throw all caution in the wind. The bloody bitch was going to ruin his life. He knew it, he could feel that she was not going to give up. Unable to sit down any longer Alan got up and stomping about in his study he gave the filing cabinet a kick, which hurt his foot, and slammed the door to the study shut. The loud bang of the closing door pulled him up, and taking a few deep breaths, went back to his desk and sat down.

'Steady now,' he told himself, 'Calm down, don't let it get to you.' He should have answered her letter making it clear that he was not going back to her, that it was over, finished and to leave him alone. Yeah, that should have nipped it in the bud. But maybe it was not too late. This nonsense will have to stop and stop right now and Alan switched the computer on. While he waited he read the letter again and when he came to: *You love me too, you have told me this more than once* Alan shrugged. Probably said it in the heat of the moment. She shouldn't have taken it seriously. The computer was ready and Alan began:

Saskia

It is with regret that - -

Alan stopped and looked at it. 'No,' he said half aloud to himself, shaking his head, 'it is not with regret, and he deleted it. And better be direct, don't beat around the bush. So there is no doubt as to what I mean.'

Saskia

I want you to stop writing to me or try to contact me in any other way.

Alan read it, 'yes' he nodded that I think it is direct enough for starters. Anyway, just in case I will add this:

Whatever you thought, or have been thinking there is nothing between us, not now, not ever before. I am sorry if that is the impression I gave you. Now please, I am asking you

and to make doubly sure she understood Alan changed to capitals, imagining this women still carrying on when Emma came home:

LEAVE ME ALONE! I DO NOT LOVE YOU. I NEVER DID, AND NEVER WILL. I DO NOT WANT TO HEAR FROM YOU AGAIN. AM I MAKING MYSELF CLEAR!

He read it. 'A bit clumsy,' he thought, but it should leave no doubt as to what he meant. He printed it and the envelope. 'Well, I hope this is the end of that,' he mumbled as he put the letter in the envelope and sealed it. After all, she is an intelligent woman and would now realise there was nothing gained by taking this any further. Alan mailed the letter on his way to work.

CHAPTER 10

Saskia's third letter arrived two days after Alan had mailed his letter to her. Too soon for it to be an answer to his letter, if indeed she was going to answer it. Alan put it on his desk and looked at it, noticing that again there was no stamp. He shook his head, she's mad, he thought, coming all this way to deliver the letter, but of course, she wants to make sure I get them. Picking it up he opened it and took out the thin piece of notepaper. It was blue this time. On the top was a little drawing of two people in an embrace.

My Dearest, dearest Alan,

Still no word from you. I am getting desperate for your company. I miss you so much. I want to have you with me. To feel your arms around me, to feel your lips on mine. To have you inside me.

Please, please contact me. I love you.
Forever yours.

Saskia Xxxxxx

Alan stared at it for a few moments shaking his head in disbelieve.

…'She's mad,' he said finally, 'The woman is mad. This is getting bloody ridiculous. It's not normal to write like that to a bloke who only came around for a bit of sex. And why the hell is she so bloody persistent. It must be bloody obvious by now that I am not going back to her. Anyway, let's hope she'll stop this nonsense when she gets my letter.'

He stuck the letter back in its envelope but as he put it in the drawer and turned the key in the lock, Alan couldn't completely shrug off the feeling that somehow his letter was not going to be the end of it. He regretted now having written the letter and a rude and clumsy letter at that. But, he reasoned, she had provoked him, writing as if he had some obligation to her. Alan shrugged, it was done now but it would have been better to have phoned her to ask her to meet him somewhere and talk about it. 'Anyway, whatever happens I am not going back to her.'

SASKIA'S DIARY

After first ignoring me and my letters he has now answered me. The hurt is terrible. I can't sleep. But I must be strong. A man came into my life. I opened my heart and took him in. He loves me. He told me that and I believed him. At last, I thought, I found real love and in that love I hoped I had found the happiness and security I longed for. I love that man so much and to have him inside me was for me the fulfilment of that love. I hoped that one day we would be together. I was soaring like a kite in the wind and suddenly I came crashing down. I have written a poem. I have never written a poem in my life but these words came through my grief:

Long hours
Did I wait for you
You never came
Slowly I decline.

SASKIA

Something you took away from me
 And you don't want to know
 Something you left behind Memory.
When the night was cold and dark
You were the warmth and the light
When the day was wet and sombre
You were the shelter and the joy.

I wait
Will you ever come?
Without you
Life is so – empty
Come back Please!
I will send this to him – soon.

CHAPTER 11

Edgy and nervous Alan waited for Saskia's answer. But when the weekend came and went and still there was no word from her Alan, once more, began to relax, reassuring himself that after receiving his letter she must have realized that whatever she thought was between them didn't exist. Now he could get on with his life and look after Emma. He only now realized how Saskia and her letters had occupied his mind. It was a great relief and he was generally in a much happier mood now when visiting Emma.

For a few days now Emma had noticed the changed in him and when one afternoon Alan was joking and laughing, Emma just had to ask: "What has happened to you? You seem much happier. Did you win the lottery?"

"No, no, it's nothing like that. I'm just so happy to see you making such good progress," Alan lied, "That makes me feel good."

Emma nodded, she could understand that. However she had been making good progress for over a week now and it seemed to have only caught up with him for the past few days. Emma shrugged, anyway it was good to see him so happy. Alan had been very quiet and withdrawn lately.

"Well, the doctor is happy and who knows I might be coming home soon and then just go for treatment to the hospital. Also they need the beds. Every once in a while somebody will tell me how desperately short of beds they are. I'm sure there is no malice in it but they're letting me know just the same."

"Well, to have you back home will be absolutely fantastic," Alan said enthusiastically, "And the sooner the better." Alan was genuinely pleased, especially now he had managed to get rid of Saskia.

On the Friday morning of that week Alan went to the nature strip, picked up his newspaper and as he turned around saw, with a heart stopping jolt the familiar small lilac envelope sticking out of the letterbox. For a few moments he stared at it as if hypnotised, then he snatched it out of the slot and resisting the urge to open it there, hurried inside and slammed the door shakily and he tore at the envelope and took out a small sheet of white notepaper. There was nothing written on it. Frowning he turned it over. Nothing. Blank. 'The bloody bitch had sent him a blank piece of paper. What the hell was she playing at now? That bloody bitch, the bloody fucking bitch. Leave me alone,' Alan shouted furiously at the piece of paper. 'I don't want to have anything to do with you anymore. It's finished, we're finished. There was never any bloody thing in the first place. Read my letter. I don't love you. I never did. Get out of my bloody life!'

Having vented his anger Alan calmed down and went upstairs to his study. He opened the drawer and put the envelope with the blank piece of paper on top of the other ones. As he did so it suddenly occurred to him that she could have been watching him taking her letter out of the letterbox because it could only have been delivered this morning. Maybe she was still out there, watching. He went onto the balcony but there was nothing unusual and out of place. Alan went back to his study, sat down at his desk and broodingly wondered how to deal with this because it was obvious now she was not going to give up. And it was equally obvious that his letter had not had the effect he had hoped for. Alan looked at the clock above his desk. The time didn't register immediately but when it did, Alan swore: 'Bloody hell,' he shouted, '20 past bloody eight and I'm still in my bloody dressing gown. I haven't even had breakfast and I should have been on the road over half an hour ago. This bloody woman was taking control of his bloody life again …..'I won't let you, I won't let you, do you hear'; he shouted, once more giving vent to his frustration because of his inability to cope with it.

He went to the bedroom, tossed his dressing gown and pyjamas onto the bed and went to have a shower; his mind a jumble of thoughts all involving Saskia. While getting dressed he was still thinking about Saskia. He shook his head, nonplussed. She seemed so nice, a real lady.

And this had been one of the things that had attracted him to her. But what for Alan had meant a bit of sex and fun had obviously meant something very different to her. He realized now only too well that she had been very serious indeed when she proposed he move in with her. And she probably had been thinking about that for some time because she would not have thought of it on the spur of the moment.

But what could he do about her now, he wondered, as he entered the garage. There was gnawing at his insides, this nagging thought that this blank piece of paper wasn't the end but the beginning of a very nasty period in his life.

Alan was beginning to hate Saskia.

CHAPTER 12

Alan had gone to see Emma. He hadn't meant to, not until the afternoon but, instead of driving through to his office in North Sydney, Alan, involuntarily, had turned left into Reserve Road leading to the hospital car park. He only realized where he was when he hit the first speed bump.

Bodily he had been in the car, his driving automatic on roads he knew like the back of his hand. But his mind had been on Saskia, the blank piece of paper and its meaning. But more importantly, and this was his greatest fear, what was she going to do next because he was sure she wouldn't send him a blank piece of paper and disappear out of his life? And mixed through all these thoughts was Emma, his wife of twenty six years, who had, apart from being his companion, friend and love, also been his counsellor, the trusted person who, with her quiet, logical and practical answers to his problems made things that seemed unsurmountable, either go away altogether, or made them seem not bad at all.

With his mind on the problems he had, without realizing it, gone to the only person who, he knew, could get him out of this mess or make it look less bad, until the speed bump brought him back to reality. This was one problem he could not talk about to Emma. This time she could not help him. When he got to the roundabout at the entrance to the car park he slowed down. He could drive around and back to the main road, but again, and seemingly beyond his control Alan drove into the car park. Finding a space on the second floor Alan parked his car and while on his way to Emma he was still wondering why he had gone to see her. But he knew why, he wanted her help. But then, the very thing he wanted her help with he could not talk about. 'I'd be a bit stupid to say: 'I've had an affair and I've broken it off. But she won't leave me alone and making my life hell. She even wants me to move in with her. What can I do about it?'

And another thing he now remembered Emma had told him that in the mornings her friends would come and as much as she liked to see him at any time of the day, could he please leave the mornings to her friends.

As he approached Emma's room Alan hesitated. Stupid, afraid to go and see your sick wife in the hospital. He should be able to go and see his wife any time of the day without worrying whether she had friends with her or not, he thought in a moment of belligerence. But he knew very well why he felt uneasy this time. This time he hadn't come to cheer her up and pass the time of day.

Saskia had got under his skin so deeply he felt totally unable to cope with this by himself. And not only for help to fight off this woman who was a threat to their happiness, but also to absolve him from his guilt for having been unfaithful to her. He stepped quietly inside and looked at Emma reading newspapers.

Emma, sensing another person in the room and seeing Alan standing there her eyebrows went up and smiling broadly she exclaimed, "Oh Darling, how lovely to see you.

"I wasn't expecting you at all." She pushed the newspaper aside, "Come here, come and sit down. Have you got time? Shouldn't you be at the office?"

Walking towards Emma, Alan gave her a weak smile in answer to her questions, kissed her and sat down, his face showing the misery he felt within.

Looking at him a bit more closely Emma, frowning worriedly said: "Are you alright Alan? Is there something the matter? You look pale and I also think you've lost weight. Are you eating well? Are you having plenty of rest? You're still not working all day and half the night, are you?"

"Er - ," Alan hesitated, glanced at Emma and then slumped and looked down at his knees. He wanted desperately to tell Emma what he had done and what it had developed into. Tell her about the letters and especially about the blank piece of paper and what she could mean by that. Tell her he was sorry, very sorry he had done this to her.

The pain of his thoughts were almost visible on his face with Emma getting really worried; she didn't know what to think. Had he lost his job? Or was he sick?

Then Alan straightened up; he must tell her and looking at Emma said: "No, no, I'm alright. It's – is – well – there is this" Alan took a deep breath, "Darling, I love you very much, you know that, but, with a sigh Alan continued, "well, there is this –"

"Oh good morning Mrs H," the young nurse said breezily rolling her trolley with medication into the room. "Oh, good morning Mr Henderson, I'm sorry for barging in like this. But it's time for your medication. And I wasn't expecting any visitor this early."

"It's alright, Ann."

"How do you feel this morning, Mrs H?"

"I'm fine, Ann"

"Bye Mrs. H. Mr Henderson" and with that the nurse wheeled her trolley back into the corridor.

Emma looked at Alan wondering now what it was he had been about to tell her, when they got interrupted.

But Alan stood up. For him the magic moment of telling Emma about Saskia and what had been happening since and to ask her what to do about it, had gone. And with that came the thought that he now should not burden Emma with his worries and problems and certainly not this one. First she had to get back to full health. Alan sighed, he would have to work this one out by himself.

"I think I'd better go" he said, worried and tormented by the uncertainty of what Saskia might do next. He put on a brave face, "Please don't worry about me, darling. It's just something at work. I just came by to tell you I love you very much, and he bent down to kiss her.

"Now, and don't you worry about me Alan, Emma said. "I'm making very good progress and unless there are complications, and doctor doesn't think there will be any, I may even be coming home within the next couple of weeks."

"That's fantastic. That is good news" Alan said, feigning enthusiasm, "I'm very happy about that." Thinking: 'Oh my God, Emma going to collect the mail and finding a lilac envelope.'

At the door he turned, waved and was gone.

For a little while after Alan had left Emma thought about what she thought he had been about to tell her when he was interrupted by the nurse. Something about a woman.

Something at work. Maybe to do with his secretary. Alan was not easy to work with. For a few more moments Emma thought about this. Then she nodded, 'yes, most likely something about his secretary. He used to talk to her about his frustrations at the office. O well' she said, 'I'll hear it one day' and putting it out of her mind, picked up the newspaper.

CHAPTER 13

Putting some letters on his desk to be signed Liza looked searchingly at Alan: "Alan, are you alright?" she asked. "You look pale and I think you have lost weight as well. Are you eating properly and are you sleeping well?"

"I'm alright Liza, thank you" Alan said. Trying not to answer, too tartly partly for having been subjected to comment about his appearance twice today.

"How is Mrs Henderson?" Liza asked after a slight pause, a bit taken aback by Alan's rather curt answer, thinking that she may have over-stepped the mark by commenting on his appearance.

"Emma is doing fine Liza, making good progress," Alan answered more amiable, glad to be able to make amends for his earlier curt answer.

'I have got to watch myself,' Alan thought, Liza has been in and out of his office a few times and he had noticed her looking at him, frowning. He realized now that he had been sitting at his desk staring into space, thinking about Saskia, and wondering what she was going to do next.

The letter was there on the morning of the fifth day and like the others; it was half sticking out of his letterbox.

A jolt of unease went through him as he took it out and halfway back to his front door he remembered he hadn't picked up his paper. He went back and as he bent down to pick it up he stealthily looked left and right to see if she was there watching. But if she was she was well hidden. Once back inside he went up to his study and opened it.

My Dearest Alan,

You saw my letter of the 16th. That is how I am! That was how I felt and still feel after getting your letter. EMPTY!! SOULLESS!! How can you do this to me? Life without you has no meaning for me. You gave me hope. You gave me life. What am I to do now Alan? Tell me, please tell me. I love you Alan. Don't you understand what that means? I wrote you a little poem. I think it says better than anything else how I feel:

Long hours
Did I wait for you
You never came
Slowly I decline.

Something you took away from me
And you don't want to know
Something you left behind
Memory!

When the night was cold and dark
You were the warmth and the light
When the day was wet and sombre
You were the shelter and the joy.

I wait
Will you ever come?
Without you
Life is so empty
Come back
Please!

Forever Yours
Saskia
Xxooo

Alan put it on his desk and looked at it for a long time. Occasionally shaking his head, not knowing whether to laugh or cry. What was the matter with the woman? Couldn't she take 'no' for an answer? How the hell could he make her understand that he had absolutely no feelings for her? The attraction had been purely sexual. And now this stupid poem. And what hope was she talking about? The woman was sick, insane. A shiver of fear went through him as he suddenly realized that if she really was, that that would make it worse. How would he be able to reason with someone like that? He read the poem again and when coming to the last verse he said, raising his voice: 'And I am not coming back. Do you understand? I am not coming back. Not now, not ever.' Alan was shouting now. 'Leave me alone, get lost, disappear. I don't want to have anything more to do with you.' Having vented his anger. Alan, calming down, reflected on the turn his philandering had taken.

Never in his wildest dreams could he have foreseen all this. For a moment, and the thought took him by surprise; Alan felt almost sorry for Saskia. He had, solely to satisfy his own ego, recklessly played with Saskia's emotions and of course she was upset and disappointed the way it had turned out. But why not let go? It had to be clear to her by now that he wasn't going to see her anymore. And that there was nothing to gain by writing those letters. Why make both their lives miserable? Alan just could not understand.

Having lost his appetite Alan locked up, got in his car and left for work. That afternoon visiting Emma; Alan tried to be cheerful but could not quite make it. He held Emma's hand as he answered her questions and engaged with her in small talk while his mind was on Saskia. Suddenly there was a silence with Emma looking at him, frowning, searchingly.

"Is there something the matter, Alan?" Emma said. "For days now, especially lately you've come to see me and I can tell. Your body might be here but your mind is not. What is it? Tell me."

"What? Er-er – sorry – um. Oh er – no, nothing. There is nothing, nothing in particular. Just a few things at the office." Alan smiled. "No, really Emma, nothing for you to worry about, really. I shouldn't be thinking about it while I am with you. I should leave the office problems where they belong, in the office. You just concentrate on getting better and I am just so happy to see you doing so well. And I promise, next time I will be there in mind and body." Alan smiled and leant over to kiss Emma. "Bye my darling. See you tomorrow."

CHAPTER 14

Waiting for Saskia's next letter, because he was sure there would be one, made Alan nervous and irritable when visiting Emma. He had to consciously keep himself in check not to snap at her. At work he sometimes forgot and impatiently would snap at staff.

Since her last letter Alan had got up every morning at around 5.30 am to watch the street until he saw his paper being delivered. Then he would go to pick it up, look at his mailbox, even open it to see if it had slipped inside. On the 5th day after the last one the letter was sticking out of the slot and Alan still had no idea when it got in there. Apart from a few cars which hadn't stopped, a few walkers and joggers, none of them had looked like Saskia, nobody else had come past his gate and Alan decided that she had to come late at night or before 5 in the morning.

'I am dammed if I am going to stay up all night,' Alan thought. 'Stuff her' and went inside and up to his study to open it.

My dearest, loving Alan,

Sorry for the delay. Don't get so upset when my letter is a bit late in coming. I know you are looking forward to them so much.

'Now, how the bloody hell?,' Alan wondered, 'did she no, she didn't, she couldn't know. The bloody bitch is guessing.'

But I wish you would come to see me. I miss you so much. I love you. My whole body is aching for your touch. I know you're married but that never stopped you coming to see me before. And the way you were with me, so beautiful, so loving that I thought you would rather be with me than with your wife.

Oh damn, I almost forgot. You see, I got carried away telling you how beautiful and loving it was being together. Anyway, I talked to your secretary. What a sweet person. And so efficient. I told her I was an old friend of the family and I had misplaced your home phone number, and could she give it to me. 'I'm sorry' she said, 'but I have to clear it with Mr Henderson.' You have her well trained Alan. Were you going to train me like that? I would have liked that. Oh – er – I haven't told her how I became an old friend of the family – Yet!

All my love Saskia

Alan stared at the letter for some time, re-reading parts of it. Frowning, puzzled. She still wanted him to come back to her, but it was different. The tone was different, cheeky, teasing, mocking him. Thinking about it Alan suddenly felt more threatened by this letter than any of the others. It was clear she was not going to let him go. She had something in mind. Alan shook his head, never expecting this sort of behaviour from her. 'You never really know people,' he thought, 'even when you have a relationship, even intimate. Often there is a facet in their character that surfaces when things don't go as planned and it is usually nasty. Well, anyway, whatever. This letter writing had to stop one way or another. And certainly before Emma came home. But how!

'Writing another letter would be useless. No, the only way he would have a good chance would be to give her a ring and arrange a meeting. It didn't matter much where as long as it was not in her apartment.' As he unlocked the bottom drawer and put the letter on top of the others he wondered if Saskia really had got onto Liza. 'No, Liza would have told him. It was all bluff, winding him up.' But it occurred to Alan how much he was thinking about her, thinking and worrying what she would do next. It suddenly dawned on him that she was in control. She knew she was and was making sure he understood.

CHAPTER 15

For a while nothing much seemed to be happening next door. At least not that Ingrid was aware of and she had been keeping an eye on it whenever she could spare the time. One thing was certain, the businessman had not been back to see her. But then, one evening, Ingrid noticed a man arriving and after a brief conversation Saskia let him in. Ingrid was livid. Now Saskia was showing her true colours, the dirty whore. How dare she use the building, their building, as a brothel? Next she'll get her mates in and then it would be really on. Ingrid was getting so upset and so angry that right now she could easily put her hands around Saskia's neck and slowly squeeze the life out of her. 'Wait till I tell Alice,' Ingrid said, half aloud to herself and she was right. She always said Saskia wouldn't give it up.

They were getting into Ingrid's car to go to Cremorne to see a movie. It was a movie they both would like to see and having missed it several times, the only place the movie was showing now was at the Cremorne Picture Theatre.

"And it's a good drive for the car, I've got to keep it going, Ingrid said, adding. "It'll only deteriorate if I just let it sit in the garage. And of course I like to keep my hand in, in driving."

"I like your car" Alice said, as Ingrid eased the car out of the car park onto the road. "Lovely car to ride in, very comfortable, leather seats and all that. Must have cost you a packet."

Ignoring Alice's observation Ingrid said: "I think you were right about Saskia. It looks like the whore has gone back to her old ways. I think she's got over the businessman not turning up anymore. Men have been calling and a few times I've seen her coming home in the morning from wherever. She's been looking very pleased with herself. It certainly looks like she's gone back to work."

Alice shrugged: "She probably needs the money. Whatever she had in mind with the businessman is gone, but yes, we can't have that, that's disgusting, and we have to do something about it."

"Yes, but what?" Ingrid said.

"Well, we could try talking to her, explaining our situation, like that we are uncomfortable with all these men turning up. Maybe sound out other people in the building. Oh, I don't know."

"I don't think we'll get very far with that," Ingrid answered, coming off the Harbour Bridge and turning into Military Road. "People today don't care. The attitude will be, it's got nothing to do with us or anybody else for that matter. As long as she doesn't set fire to the place or blow it up, it's none of our business."

"Well," Alice persisted, "if she doesn't listen, we'll talk to Glenda. It's not right all these men hanging around. Single, elderly women in the building could feel threatened by this."

"Yes OK, but what do you think she can do about it?" Ingrid answered. "I'm sure she'll say 'she bought the apartment and she's entitled to have visitors.' No Alice, there is nothing we can do about it. Anyway, let's forget about it now. Let's go and see the movie."

CHAPTER 16

Ever since getting Saskia's letter Alan hadn't been himself. It had unsettled him more than he would like to admit and he couldn't stop thinking about it. At work he would just sit at his desk and stare. At home, even with the T.V. on he found he hadn't seen anything for the past 15 minutes or so. He had trouble sleeping and even when visiting Emma, his mind kept drifting off to Saskia and the letter.

What had alarmed and upset him most was the sarcastic, mocking tone of the letter. The letters with her desperate plea to have him come back to her he could cope with. He wasn't going back and that was it. He also had been quietly confident that she would wake up to the fact that she was wasting her time writing those letters and stop them and forget about him. But this letter, the way it was written, was telling him that she was not going to let things go.

It was four days now since the letter and it was still upsetting him. One morning coming in with his cup of coffee Liza, frowning at Alan, asked: "Is everything alright Alan? You look very pre-occupied and worried. I don't want to pry but is Mrs Henderson alright?"

Alan looked at Liza, thinking: 'You've got to stop thinking about this bloody letter. Get a grip on yourself. Ignore it.' Then he sighed and said: "Emma is dong reasonably well but we're waiting on some more test results and that is a bit of a worry. I'm sorry it showed but I can't help thinking about it.

"Of course you're thinking about it," Liza said, "and at a time like this you should be with Mrs Henderson. She needs you. Now, why don't you go early? If something comes up I can't handle I'll give you a ring."

"Thank you Liza," Alan smiled. "Yes, you're probably right. The way I am at present I'm not much good here anyway. I appreciate this very much. I want you to know that. I'll clear up a few things now and I'll be off."

"Please give my regards to Mrs Henderson and wish her a speedy recovery from me" Liza said.

"I will, thank you Liza."

On his way to Emma, Alan resolved to phone Saskia as soon as possible to make a date to get together. It didn't matter so much where as long as it was not in her apartment, Alan was confident that when and if he had a chance to talk to her they would be able to come to an agreement. She was an intelligent woman and Alan was sure he could persuade her to stop all this. Alan felt better now. He had a plan. But still with Saskia on his mind he saw Emma.

Frowning, Emma said: "Alan, there is something worrying you. Now, what is it?"

"Nothing, nothing really," Alan lied, shaking his head and pulling a face to emphasize his denial.

When Emma didn't say anything, but kept looking at him, Alan added: "Well, you know, I'm worried about you and how much longer you have to be in here."

"But Alan," Emma said, gently chiding him. "I only told you a few days ago that I am doing well and that the doctor is very happy with my progress. I could even be going home in maybe 10 days or so."

"Yes, er – I mean, no of course I haven't forgotten that. I didn't think of it just now." Alan answered, a bit miffed.

"Anyway, being at home will be a lot easier on you and Marjorie. Did you know she comes to see me every second or third day? She really is a very good friend."

"Yes" Alan agreed, "she is a good friend, thinking '10 days.' He had to somehow stop Saskia writing those letters, and soon. "It'll be fantastic to have you home again, Alan said with feint enthusiasm. "It can't happen soon enough. You know, it's been very lonely without you. Well, my darling. I think I'll leave you now and let you have some rest. And I'll see you again tomorrow." Bending over to kiss Emma, Alan said: "I love you very much."

Smiling up at Alan; Emma squeezed his hand, "I know, and I love you very much."

"OK, bye now, see you tomorrow." 'Stupid twit' Alan admonished himself on his way back to the car. 'It's been lonely without you,' he mocked. Emma hadn't let on but she must have thought of the many times she had been left by herself because of his

.........he didn't want to remind himself about that period in his life.

On arriving home Alan went straight to the mailbox; a few bills but nothing from Saskia. Strange, he thought, frowning, pausing a moment in front of the letterbox; there should have been one because he had noticed some sort of pattern, 4-5 days. As he put the car away in the garage he was angry with himself for even rationalizing it. The bloody woman was in charge of his mind. It had even got to the stage that, when he saw something lilac, his heart did a double take.

Once inside he poured himself a scotch, went upstairs into his study and he nearly dropped his scotch. There it was, lying on the centre of his deskpad, the familiar small lilac envelope. Staring at it as if hypnotised it took a few moments for the shock to settle, then he grabbed it, downed his scotch and crumbling the letter into a ball threw it across the room screaming obscenities at Saskia. In his fury he gave the metal waste-paper bin such a kick it flew across the room against the glass door of the bookcase that held his precious rare and first editions, breaking it. This pulled Alan up. Still very upset but calming, he sat down at his desk; his mind a jumble of thoughts with none making sense, but slowly getting more focused.

How had she managed to get inside the house? She didn't have a key. Breaking in! No, she wouldn't be that stupid. But to make sure Alan got up and walked around the house. When he got to the laundry and saw the washing neatly folded, shirts ironed; he realized what had happened. But that meant that the woman had come to the front door and given the letter to Mrs Miller. Alan nodded, of course, that what's happened and going back to his study he picked up the phone to ring Mrs Miller. He wanted to be sure.

"Mrs Miller?" he queried when she answered the phone. "Yes," hesitantly, suspicious.

"It's Alan Henderson, Mrs Miller. Thanks for the fine job you did with the washing and ironing. Er, did somebody call when you were here?"

"Oh, yes, Mr Henderson. I should have told you a lady came to the door, a very nice lady. She said: "I wonder if you could put this on his desk. And she gave me this letter. I told her that I would do that. Oh, Mr Henderson. I hope I did the right thing?, Mrs Miller added, worried she might have done something wrong.

"It's alright, Mrs Miller. "Don't worry. Thank you very much. Goodbye Mrs Miller."

"Goodbye Mr Henderson."

Reflectively Alan put the phone back on its station. Sighing deeply he shook his head, despairingly. Not content to just put her letters in his mailbox, now she bloody well came to the front door. But how did .....? Of course, Alan answered his own question. Mrs Miller's car would have been parked out front and she may have seen Mrs Miller going inside. Still pretty bloody brazen to come to the front door.

'Put it on his desk so he can see it when he comes in,' Alan mimicked her voice. Of course, go for the full effect. The bloody bitch had known the impact it would have on him. She obviously seemed to know him better than he knew her. Alan didn't have a clue what she was really like. But he began to get a bit of an idea. His impression of her had always been so femininely submissive and alluring and only really interested in having sex. They had never really talked, never had a serious conversation, never explored likes and dislikes, through which he could have gotten to know her.

But obviously she hadn't needed that. She must be a better judge of character than he, he who prided himself in being a better than average judge of character. It also had never occurred to Alan that she could really be in love with him. He had been too busy having sex to think of anything else, Alan thought grimly. And of course she had now began to realise that whatever she thought they had was really over and that indeed he won't be coming back to her.

Now love had turned into hate and wanted revenge and now she was on a vendetta to destroy him. Alan shook his head; he had never thought about it like that but that was obviously what was happening. He might as well forget the picture of soft femininity and charm. This woman was smart, dangerous and as hard as nails. My God what have I got myself into?

His next thought made him even more nervous. Emma would be coming home within the next 10 days or so. What if Saskia came to the front door and gave the letter to Emma? He could just see it. "Good day Mrs Henderson. I wonder if you could give this to your husband?" She might even call him Alan. Or maybe, "May I come in and talk to you. I have something very interesting to tell you about your husband."

Unable to sit calmly at his desk while these thoughts were running through his mind, Alan got up and walked around the study, through the rooms and finally onto the balcony outside the bedroom. After a few minutes, looking out over the water, Alan calmed down and went back to his desk and sat down. 'I'm bloody stupid to get myself worked up like that. It's not going to happen. But I've got to stop her writing those letters.

'Sooner or later Emma will see one of them and she'll know what's been going on. Anyway why couldn't she take no for an answer? She shouldn't have taken it so bloody serious.' For a few moments Alan looked at the scrunched up letter on the floor near the cabinet with the broken glass, then he picked it up and smoothing it out, opened it.

My Dearest Alan,

Don't you miss me? I miss you very much. It's been a long time since you've been in my arms and inside my body. I am aching for your touch. Oh – er – by the way, I have spoken to your wife. I told her how much fun we used to have in bed and how good you are. You do remember those times, don't you Alan, I do. I am very sorry about your wife being sick but I had to let her know what an absolute perfect two-timing bastard you are. Now, I don't mind that as long as you come back to me. I'm not sure if she believed me but I will tell her again when I next visit her.

All my love Forever Yours, Saskia

Alan put the letter on his desk and stared at it for a long time, occasionally shaking his head. 'She's lying,' he said at last, half aloud, 'The bloody bitch is lying. She didn't talk to Emma. Emma would have said something. Or,' Alan hesitated, 'Maybe she wouldn't, at least not just yet, giving him the benefit of the doubt. But then again?'

Actually, now he thought about it, Emma occasionally had given him the odd puzzling glance as if she was trying to work out something. He hadn't taken much notice of it at the time but now, after reading Saskia's letter it made sense. But Emma had kept her hand in his and she had kissed him warmly goodbye. But how did Saskia know Emma was in hospital? Alan was sure Liza hadn't told her. The bloody woman must have been following him.

Staring morosely ahead Alan shook his head despairingly. He didn't believe, but of course didn't know for sure, that Saskia had talked to Liza or Emma. But if she was trying to unsettle him, she was succeeding extremely well. And what was she going to do next? But more importantly, how could he stop her? He should have phoned her instead of writing that letter. He may have been able to sort something out. But what? He won't be going back to her and that seems to have been the only thing she had been interested in. Except that now Alan wasn't so sure about that anymore. There was definitely a change of tone in her letters. Apart from mocking him, it seemed that now she was out to embarrass him, and not only embarrass him but ruin his marriage and how, he wondered, was he going to stop that?

SASKIA'S DIARY

I will not ask him to come back to me anymore and I have written my last letter. I did send him my poem hoping that that would make him understand what he has done to me. But he totally ignores me. It is obvious now he didn't love me. He never did, he used me. It was only sex he was after, not love, not me.

Well, seeing he is ignoring me I got in touch with his wife. He will not get away with it. I followed him for a few days and found he goes to the North Shore Hospital every day. I phoned the hospital and they told me that his wife is there recuperating from a cancer operation. One day when he left I went to see her and had a talk to her. I felt sorry for her but I want her to know. But when I was with her I found it difficult to tell her what had happened, but I will go and see her again and I will tell her then. She must know.

CHAPTER 17

"How are you darling?" Alan said, bending down to kiss her. "You look well," he added putting a bunch of roses on the bed.

"Oh, they're lovely," Emma said, picking them up and smelling them. "A lovely thought darling, thank you. I'll get the nurse to put them in a vase. And I am well. I can feel a change in me almost every day. How are things at home?"

"Everything is fine. Mrs Miller is doing a good job keeping it ship-shape. I'm afraid the stove is not getting much use now. I usually take my meals in town or have a takeaway."

"Now, don't skimp on your meals just because I'm not there to cook them for you."

"Don't worry, I'm not. Do you get many visitors?" Alan suddenly asked. He couldn't contain himself any longer. He had to know.

Emma looked at him raising her eyebrows in surprise at the sudden change of the subject but more so at the brusqueness and urgency in the voice.

"No" she said, after a few moments, "mainly you and Marjorie, but that's alright. I've got plenty to read. Oh yes, I must tell you. A couple of days ago a young woman, late thirties I think, walked into my room. She seemed surprised on seeing me and then she realized she had gone into the wrong room. She apologized for disturbing me and then asked how I was, and from one thing came another. Actually we finished up having quite a chat. Funny now I think about it, she didn't seem in any hurry to go to the person she came to visit. Also," Emma added pensively, "somehow I had the feeling that she knew me, or at least knew about me."

"What did you talk about?" Alan demanded, almost snarling at the question.

Emma again frowned at Alan, puzzled. Then she shrugged, "Nothing in particular, the weather, the care in the hospital, how much longer I thought I would be here, just generalities, then she said she'd like to come back to see me again. I really enjoyed our little chat."

I said, "Yes, I enjoyed it too, but you don't have to." She ignored that. And then she said: "Amazing, we've been chatting away here and we don't even know each other's names."

"You can call me Sassie."

"And I am Emma."

"Hey, what's the matter dear, are you alright?" Emma asked. Worried, interrupting herself.

Although already having guessed the visitor had to be Saskia, Alan inadvertently groaned and grimaced at hearing his pet name for her. Recovering he answered brusquely, "I'm alright. It's probably something I ate. It's giving me terrible heartburn."

"Alan," Emma said, gently scolding him. "You must be careful what you eat. Don't eat out so much. Do a bit of cooking yourself. You must look after yourself."

"OK. Yes. I will, Alan answered, grateful the conversation got away from the visitor.

"I'm sorry I'm not home to look after you darling, Emma said squeezing his hand, "but let's hope I'm not going to be in here much longer. I miss you darling."

"I miss you too darling," Alan said, making an effort to be and sound normal, while inwardly seething with anger at Saskia. 'The bloody bitch had really been to see Emma."

"Alan!" The querying tone and searching look on Emma's face shook him out of his thoughts. But he was angry and upset and he had to get away. He had to think about this and see what he could do to stop her seeing Emma again. And he couldn't think straight with Emma every once in a while looking at him with that puzzled frown.

Alan grimaced and shrugged: "I am sorry Emma, it's just er – well, my stomach is really upset. I don't know what it is. I'm really sorry Emma, but I think I had better go home. The way I am I'm not much company for you anyway."

"But Alan, just you being here with me is so nice but yes, go home and take something to settle your stomach. And please Alan, be more careful in the future what you eat and where you eat it."

"Yes I will. I'm sorry darling. I really am. But I'll be back tomorrow. Bye darling." Alan bent down to kiss, a wave at the door and Alan was gone.

Long after Alan had left, Emma was still thinking about the rather odd turn of events. There were questions for which there were no answers. And as the thoughts kept milling around in her head, Emma began to feel uneasy. Worried about Alan at first about his eating, she had not immediately made the connection but as she kept thinking about it, she began to find Alan's behaviour rather strange. When he had arrived and for the best part of his visit he had been alright then, when she told him she'd had a visitor she had noticed Alan beginning to fidget in his chair. But it was only after she had told him the name of the visitor that he had become upset and had developed stomach pains. Did he know the woman? Old doubts and suspicions returned.

And had the woman come into her room really expecting someone else? And why did she want to come and see her again? What for? Just to chat? What is so special about me? And what about the person she came to visit? Why not go to that person?

Upset and confused Emma sunk back into her pillow and sighed deeply. Then there were the meetings till late at night. Unfamiliar perfume on his clothes. But she wanted to believe this was nothing. All a coincidence. He could really have an upset stomach. She wanted to believe him. She had to believe him.

For a long time Emma just lay there, thoughts tumbling through her mind. In the end she thought 'why not talk it over with Marjorie?' She'd put her right. She clearly remembered Marjorie's words when some weeks ago she had confided in her about her doubts, fears and suspicions.

"Alan!!!" Marjorie had said, "another woman!! Nah. He worships the ground you walk on. "He won't kiss me on the lips or give me a sexy cuddle because you might get upset. Alan!!! Another woman!! Ha!!"

Emma shivered involuntarily. Was she indeed just simply imagining all this? Of course she was. Alan wouldn't do anything like that. He loved her. He was her husband.

CHAPTER 18

All the way home Alan fumed about the bloody bitch getting to Emma. Not content anymore to make his life miserable, now she had to involve Emma. As he realized he couldn't stop Saskia going to Emma, a renewed wave of anger went through him.

Pre-occupied with it all Alan nearly ran into the car in front of him which had stopped at a traffic light. And the blast from a car behind reminded Alan that it had turned green and he had to keep going. But by the time he had arrived home, garaged his car, collected his mail and gone inside the house, he had calmed down. He went up to his study and after ordering a pizza poured himself a scotch and sipping it wondered what Saskia would be doing next, now having made contact with Emma. Leaning back in his chair he closed his eyes. This had now taken on a whole new perspective. Forget about the lilac envelopes and his fear of Emma seeing them. Things got a lot more complicated and confronting.

And she wants to go and see Emma again and it wouldn't be the weather they'd be talking about. Maybe if he talked to her. Alan looked at his watch. It was about the time he used to phone her. He sighed and picked up the phone and punched in Saskia's number. It rang once, twice and just as it began its third ring Alan hung up. He couldn't do it. Alan leaned back in his chair, troubled, worried. Picking up the phone and punching in her number had never been a problem and on hearing her sexy throaty voice, his body would glow and hurt with the want for her, cursing the hold-ups in Sydney traffic. But now! He was apprehensive about contacting her, wondering how she was going to react. It had been a long time and he had ignored her apart from writing that stupid letter. Alan shrugged. He'd just have to cop it, eat humble pie and say sorry. Right. Taking a deep breath Alan picked up the phone and punched in Saskia's number.

"Yes, it was answered almost immediately. Her voice was as Alan remembered it, soft and throaty. Alan hesitated, memories flooding back, his body beginning to respond.

"Who is speaking please?" The voice was different now, impatient, cold, demanding.

"Er – it's – er – I'm – I'm sorry, er – it's me, Alan," he stuttered, stumbling over his words, thrown off balance by the different in her voice.

Finally firmer, finding his composure, he said: "It's me Saskia, Alan. I would like to talk to you?"

"Alan! Alan Henderson? How nice of you to call," The voice was mocking. "What is there to talk about Alan? How you walked out of my life. How you ignored my pleas to call me. How you ruined my life? Sure, let's talk, but it won't do you much good. I am going to tell your wife, because that what this is about isn't it? Are you still there Alan? Do you still want to talk?"

"Please Saskia," Alan felt himself getting hot and he began to perspire. "I'm sorry Saskia. I was wrong, very wrong. I treated you badly and I am truly sorry about it."

"Sorry! You are sorry! Sorry about what?" Saskia flung the words at him, "Sorry that your wife is going to find out, or that you used me and ruined my life?"

Alan was beginning to get annoyed. He resented her saying that he ruined her life. 'That's a bit bloody dramatic,' he thought. How the bloody hell could he have ruined her life by not going back to her? As he was contemplating to tell her that, knowing full well that that would place any goodwill in jeopardy he heard her say:

"Anyway, I'm not going to discuss this any further. There is nothing to discuss. And furthermore, I don't want to hear from you or see you ever again."

The click in his ear terminated the conversation.

Taken aback at the abrupt ending Alan sat quite still for a few moments before replacing the hand piece. Whatever he had expected, it certainly wasn't this. But then what had he expected? Alan shrugged, had he been too optimistically naïve to think that after he had ignored her all this time; she would meekly promise to leave him and Emma alone?"

Maybe if he – he, he sighed. Maybe this or maybe that. It was a bit late but it was beginning to be very obvious now; to Alan that Saskia had been expecting a lot more from their relationship than he had even intended. And that, he was sure, was at the back of it all. He shook his head finding it difficult to equate the soft, loveable, utterly feminine woman he knew with the cold and ruthless enemy she had become. And only because he had broken off a relationship which, as far as he was concerned, had no future in the first place. To be fair she hadn't known that. But why the hell she had to be so bloody clingy now; now she knew it wouldn't ever come to anything, was beyond him.

He wouldn't have been able to keep meeting with her the way he had anyway. It had surprised him that he had been able to do this for so long without Emma getting suspicious. It was only because of Saskia's suggestion that he move in with her that had speeded things up. But for goodness sake, relationships are started and broken off all the time. One just has to get over it without making the other person suffer. Anyway, whatever, he wasn't going back to her. That period of his life was finished, never to be reopened again. His life now was with Emma. But he knew where he stood now.

He had to find another way to stop her. Emma must never find out about this period in his life. How he was going to stop her he didn't quite know. But stop her he would.

CHAPTER 19

"Hello, may I come in please?"

Emma looked up from her book to see the woman who had accidentally come into her room a few days ago standing in the doorway.

"Emma, isn't it? How are you? I'm Sassie. Do you remember me?"

"I'm fine thanks. Yes, I do remember you," Emma said, somewhat surprised that this woman was interested enough in her to come back and visit her again.

As if she had read Emma's mind, Saskia said: "Yes, I've been to see my friend and I thought while I am here I'll go and see how Emma is. I hope you don't mind?"

"No, no, of course not. But it's a pity you didn't come a bit earlier, you would have been able to meet my husband."

"Oh, I'm sorry I missed him," Saskia sounded really sorry. "Yes, that would have been interesting."

"Yes, I'm sure he would have liked to have met you. I told him about you."

"Did you? I'm sure he hadn't expected me turning up."

Emma looked at Saskia, frowning but before she could ask what she meant by that, Saskia added: "Well I must say you look a lot better than when I saw you last. Oh Emma, may I?" Saskia pulled up a chair and not waiting for an answer, sat down.

"Do you think you'll go home soon?"

"Well, it depends on what you mean by soon," Emma said. "It'll be at least another week. But I'm counting down and that is encouraging."

Saskia nodded. "Yes, that's right. And it'll be nice for Alan to have you back home again."

"Yes, he's looking forward to that very much."

Saskia nodded. "Of course. But I'm sure he comes to see you often. His office is not that far away, it's only in North Sydney, isn't it?"

It suddenly dawned on Emma that Sassie knew her husband's name and she was sure she hadn't told her that.

"Sorry," she said, "I didn't hear what you said just then."

Saskia looked at Emma, feeling terrible for being so cruel, but her hate for her husband ruled out all sympathy. Saskia wanted to hurt Alan Henderson with everything at her disposal and unfortunately this was going to involve Emma.

To begin with, as she was doing now, she would tell Emma enough to get her wondering and hopefully start asking her husband some questions and demanding some answers. Then, when she would come the third time she would tell all.

"I said," Saskia repeated, "he is not that far away from his office in North Sydney, isn't it?"

"Yes, it is," Emma said, thinking, what else does she know about my husband that I haven't told her.

"Do you get many visitors?" Saskia asked, changing the subject for a moment.

"No, not many, but I'm alright. I've got plenty to occupy myself with."

"Well, my friend's leaving the hospital very soon but I would love to come back to see you before you go home."

"That's very kind of you, but it isn't necessary" Emma didn't want her to come again, feeling uncomfortable with her presence, which she couldn't explain. But also, she didn't want to offend her.

"It's not a bother, honestly" Saskia said, "I'd like to come and see you. We've got so much to talk about."

"OK," Emma gave in but in a last effort to discourage her to come she said: "But my husband comes often and his visits are a bit unpredictable. Also my friend can turn up at any time." Thinking what it was she was going to talk about next time that she couldn't say now. She didn't even know the woman.

"Well, no problem, if they're here I won't come in. But it's very nice that Alan comes so often, because I'm sure he is a very busy man, working often till late at night. You'd think he wasn't married. Well, I must go now. It's good to see you doing so well.

"Please give my love to Alan" Saskia said getting up. "I'm sure he'll be very interested to hear that I came to see you again. Bye now."

"Don't go please." Emma straightened up and urgently began. "Can you – "

But Saskia, turning her head at the door, smiled and went, leaving Emma to finish – "please tell me how you know my husband's name is Alan," to the empty doorframe.

There were other questions like: 'How do you know his office is in North Sydney?' And, and here Emma got really upset, 'what do you know about his late evening meetings?"

Uncertain, distraught and close to tears Emma sunk back against the pillows. As she did she took in another whiff of Saskia's still lingering perfume.

Frowning, coming upright again Emma sniffed again. It was vaguely familiar. She had smelled it before, but where? As soon as she had asked herself that Emma knew, on Alan's clothes after he came home from his late night meetings. Emma could still remember, thinking 'Oh well, there are women on the board.' And Emma now remembered too that, after Saskia first visited she had been thinking: 'I've smelt that perfume before, but at that time not being suspicious of anything, had not given it a second thought.

'You've been a fool' Emma berated herself angrily, 'a stupid, trusting bloody fool. There were no meetings except with this woman.' Alan's behaviour made much more sense now after she had told him a woman called Sassie had accidently visited her.

'Accidentally! My foot! Pain in his stomach. What rot'

Emma was getting more angrier as she thought about it. 'And this woman! How dare she come in here and gloat.' Emma got herself so upset she couldn't lie in bed any longer. She got out of bed, put on her dressing gown and went into the corridors pacing up and down.

The words: 'Give my love to Alan,' kept on tumbling through her mind. 'The bloody cheek of her'

After walking up and down the corridor for a few times Emma calmed down somewhat and went back to bed. She thought of ringing Marjorie but then she thought that it may not be a good idea to talk about this over the phone. Also, it was well after 4 o'clock and Alan could turn up any time now.

'What should she do?' Emma wondered nervously. Confront him with it, hint at it or not let on she knew about this Sassie and his late night meetings? And how should she behave knowing what she knows now? Emma hoped he wouldn't come. She needed time to think. Emma was sure now that the woman's visit had not been accidental. 'She had come to see whom she was up against, like, look at me. You got no chance. Alan is mine.'

Emma was working herself into a state. 'How could this woman be so cruel? And Alan, her Alan, could he be part of this?' Tears welled up in her eyes; it had to be. 'How else would this woman know she was in hospital and in which room? How could he do this to her? They really picked this moment. No wonder the woman was trying to work out when she was leaving hospital? The bloody bitch.' Emma had never, and would never call anybody a bloody bitch. It was not in her nature. But now she was so upset, so disappointed and so angry, her usual gentleness had been set aside.

'I've been right all along,' Emma thought, 'right from when she had first voiced her suspicions to Marjorie.' She looked at her watch, half past four. Emma eased back into the pillow and closed her eyes. 'Relax.' She told herself, 'don't let it get to you. Get better first. Getting worked up like this won't do your body any good.' But she would talk to Marjorie about the latest ---'

"And how is my lovely wife?" There he was, in the room, big grin on his face and a bunch of lilies in his hand.

"I'm fine" Emma was unintentionally short.

"Hey, what's the matter, what happened?" Alan's grin disappeared and his face dropped, "have you had bad news? Has something come up? What is it, tell me?" The concern and urgency in his voice were genuine.

"No, it's nothing like that. I'm fine, really."

"What is it then? Tell me, Alan demanded impatiently, his buoyant mood gone. Emma hesitated, feeling terrible and sick to the stomach.

"Well, OK then" she said finally, nervously trying to look Alan in the eyes but in the end she couldn't do that. "Do you know this woman called Sassie who came to visit me the other day?"

The question took Alan by surprise. He hadn't expected this and certainly not put so directly.

Taken aback Alan hesitated and for a few moments his eyes glanced at an object above Emma, then, lowering them, looking grimly at Emma, he answered in a chipped: "No."

"Well, she seems to know you," Emma said, almost apologetically. Sorry now she had brought it up. It could have waited.

"That's possible," Alan answered tersely, "I meet a lot of people through my work but I can't remember everybody I come into contact with."

Emma was on the verge of saying, 'Not even a beautiful lady like Sassie' but Alan, getting more agitated continued, raising his voice: "Look, I came to visit you to talk about us and you want to know if I know some bloody tart who happens to blunder into your room. Maybe I'd know her when I see her but the name means nothing to me."

Still believing Alan was lying and he knew the woman but thinking 'this is not the time or the place to pursue this, Emma said conciliatorily: "I'm sorry, of course you can't remember everybody you come into contact with. So how's work?" she added, brightly.

Nervously seething, Alan sat down. 'The bloody woman! Wonder what she has told Emma?' Pulling his chair a bit closer Alan took Emma's hand. She stiffened but didn't pull back.

Composing himself, Alan pulled a face and shrugged: "Work," he said, "it's alright. But lately my mind has not been on the job one hundred per cent. My mind is more on you, on us and how good it will be to have you back home again."

At this point Emma didn't know what to think anymore. 'If he is involved with this woman; then why is he so eager and happy to have me back home?' she thought. And doubts about the woman's honesty began to surface. 'She wanted so much to believe Alan had nothing to do with her and the woman was just mischief-making. But then there was the perfume, her knowing about the late night meetings she wanted to ask him about that.

"Anyway," Alan said cheerfully, cutting into Emma's thoughts. "I think we should go for a big long holiday. Let's take a trip through Europe, go to some of those famous cities like Vienna, Budapest, Amsterdam or Rome. I've always wanted to go there.

"Well, of course you will have to be strong enough to travel. I suppose I'll have to fatten you up a bit first, and that'll put a strain on my cooking skills for sure."

Alan stopped talking. He could see Emma was only half-listening, her mind obviously on what Saskia had been telling her. He could barely control his anger but he realized it would make matters worse if he made a scene.

'Ignore it,' he counselled himself, 'just keep going as if it doesn't concern me.' He was going to say, 'don't believe any of what she has been telling you' but he checked himself in time. That would all but admit that he knew Saskia.

"Listen Emma," he began again with feigned enthusiasm, "What I wanted to tell you was that the herb garden you put in is doing fine, Alan said, thinking, 'I've got to get her mind off that bloody Saskia. '

"You know I'm not much of a gardener, but I managed to keep them alive. I know how proud you were when you got it going and I don't want them dying on my watch. I put the drip on a couple of times and that seemed to be all they need."

Emma was looking at him but he wondered if she had heard what he had said.

But then Emma nodded: "Oh, that's nice that they're doing so well." It was said without enthusiasm but Alan sat back and sighed, at least she had been listening.

After an embarrassing and awkward silence Alan, racking his brain to find something else, he thought she would be interested in, finally said as cheerful as he could manage: "Oh yes, er, Mrs Miller is doing a great job in keeping the house neat and tidy. Not that there is much to do but she also does the washing and ironing. She comes twice a week and I think we should keep her on when you're back home."

"I don't think that is necessary," Emma answered rather gruffly. "I can do it."

"Maybe you can. But I think it is best if we keep Mrs Miller on," Alan insisted, trying hard not to lose his temper.

Emma, not interested in having an argument about it, pulled a face and shrugged, "We'll see."

"Well, that's settled then," Alan forced a smile. This was not a good visit and as much as he wanted to leave; he didn't want to go in this atmosphere and tension.

"You have plenty to read I see?" Alan said gesturing at the four paperback novels on her bedside table. "Did Marjorie bring them?"

Emma nodded, "Yeah."

Realising he could stay with her for the rest of the day and trying to dream up all sorts of things to say, things would not improve. If anything, it could get worse. Saskia had really managed to get to her.

"Well, my darling," Alan said cheerfully, getting up, refusing to react to her grumpy mood. "You're looking very well and I'm looking forward to having you back home again. And now I think I had better be going. But I'll be back tomorrow."

As Alan bent to kiss Emma; his hand went to her breasts, lightly stroking them. Taking her completely by surprise it sent a shock through her. It had been a long time since Alan had done anything like that. The shock was pleasurable and she almost put her hands on his wanting them to stray there. But Emma didn't. She couldn't. There was too much that was unexplained.

Alan straightened up, smiling and at the door he turned around, waved and was gone.

Emma sunk back in the pillows, worried, uncertain. His hands on her breasts had upset her more than she wanted to admit. The surge through her body had been the want, the need for him to make love to her. To tell her, 'I love you. You're the only one.' Emma wanted to believe that. She wanted so much to believe he didn't know the woman. But there was this doubt; this nagging inner voice that told her: 'he does know her, everything you've heard and seen points that way. That he doesn't admit it makes it worse.'

Hanging onto the last straw that had entered her head was that the woman was trying to discredit Alan. Some sort of blackmail. She could be from another firm losing clients. And of course she would know about his meetings and seminars. She probably was at some of them. Thinking about that now it amazed Emma that she had never asked what was there and what it was about. Not once had she done that. And Alan never talked about it. And also it could be misconstrued, like not trusting him, checking up on him.

And just now too, his denial had been very convincing and his anger had been genuine. His concern about her recuperation had touched her 'and that too,' Emma felt, 'has been genuine.' Sighing deeply, emotionally exhausted and now more confused than before, Emma closed her eyes and tried not to think of anything.

CHAPTER 20

Ingrid Freeman still exercised. Once a fortnight on a Tuesday afternoon a workout in the gym. Wednesday was her golf day. She still managed 18 holes and the Saturday morning was often set aside for a game of tennis. Occasionally she would ask Alice to come with her, at least to the gym but Alice declined. Alice had never been to a gym, played golf and tennis and, she had told Ingrid: "I'm certainly not going to start now. Heaven knows, at my age, I might drop dead."

This Tuesday after a workout at the gym, Ingrid had run into an acquaintance she had not seen for some time and they had coffee together. Coming home much later than usual she noticed, while getting out of the taxi across from the apartment, the businessman leaning on a car, looking at the building. The car, she noticed, was a large silver Lexus. Seeing him, a tingling went through her body and a desire that had not been there while she had not seen him, returned.

'What,' Ingrid wondered, 'is he doing there watching the apartments. Obviously it had to do with Saskia but if he wants to talk to the woman, why doesn't he just knock on her door. But what on earth does he see in her? If he only knew what went on in her apartment. Somebody should tell him she's nothing but a common whore.'

As soon as she got home she phoned Alice; Ingrid said excitedly, "You won't believe who is across the road watching the building?"

"Well," Alice answered drily, "seeing you're so excited about it, I'd say it's the businessman."

Ingrid laughed: "Right first time. Mind if I come up? Have you got a pair of binoculars?"

"No, I haven't and please come up."

"OK. I'll bring a pair of binoculars. You can have a good look at him then."

Standing next to Alice at the window Ingrid said: "See that silver car across the road, that's his. Look he's gone back inside the car again. You wonder what's going on?"

"Maybe he wants to come back?" Alice ventured. "OK, but why doesn't he just knock on her door?"

"Maybe he's checking upon her to see what she is up to?" Alice said, "but you wonder now who has given the boot to whom."

"Yes. You wonder, it's very - - -, Oh, there he is," Ingrid said excitedly, "he's just got out of his car, here" and handing Alice the binoculars, she added: "have a good look at him."

"Oh yes, he is good looking," Alice said. "Oh, I wouldn't mind."

"Wouldn't mind what?" Ingrid frowned at Alice, thinking 'he wouldn't want you, you uncouth, uncivilized Philistine. Come to think of it you don't belong here either but at least you're not a whore.'

Alice smiled, "Nothing," she said, the binoculars firmly trained on the businessman. "Yes, you wonder what he is doing. Do you think he'd be back tomorrow?"

"Your guess is as good as mine," Ingrid said, "but maybe you can keep an eye out for him. Could you let me know if he turns up again? Well, OK, then, I'll leave you to it," thinking 'I didn't think you had it in you,' "and – er – keep the binoculars for a while. They will come in handy. See you later. I'll let myself out."

Wednesday evening, Alice phoned Ingrid. 'The businessman is across the road again. I'm sure it's him."

"Thanks for telling me. Did you notice what time he left yesterday?"

"No, I didn't. But he was still there at 9.30 when I went to bed."

"It's very strange, this whole thing."

"Yes, it is, Alice said, "I'm itching to go down to ask him what he is doing. This has really got me intrigued. I mean, here he is, sitting in his car watching, and you'd think all he has to do is go up to her apartment and knock on her door."

"Yes indeed," Ingrid said, "and if he doesn't want to do that why doesn't he just phone and ask her to see him?"

"Well, it could be he suspects she's gone back to her old ways and he wants to catch her out," Alice offered.

"Do you think he knew?" Ingrid asked incredibly.

"Well, if he did he'd be pretty stupid to get involved with her. And anyway, what is it to him now what she is doing?" Alice answered.

"Maybe he's in love and he wants her back?" Ingrid said.

"Well, that brings me back to what I said before. We don't know what's going on and we'll keep going around in circles guessing. Anyway, I'll be in touch. Have a nice evening. Bye," And Alice hung up.

Ingrid had just finished setting the table for her dinner when her phone rang.

"It's me, Alice," she heard when she picked it up. "He's just arrived. I don't know what you want to do but this is the last time I'm watching. It's too stupid for words and I really don't care anymore," Alice ended aggressively.

"OK. OK. I agree," Ingrid said, "don't get your knickers in a knot. Yes, it is stupid and yes, we'll forget about it after tonight. Let's meet up tomorrow and have a cup of coffee, my place, your place or somewhere else. We'll talk about it tomorrow. Bye now."

Alice had settled in front of the TV. At least she would not be wasting the evening watching this stupid man looking at the building. When there was an ad, Alice would go to the window, pick up the binoculars and have a look.

He was either standing on the footpath or sitting in his car. At one time she saw him going in his car and Alice waited, thinking that he might be going. But when, after some time it was obvious he wasn't, Alice went back to her movie. When she got there the ads had finished and the next segment of the film was on its way. Annoyed, she sat down not knowing how long it had been going for and what she had missed when the next lot of ads came onto the screen. 'My God, I've missed a whole segment. This damn man and his whore. I should forget about it. What do I care what he is doing?" But she knew she would keep looking.

Curiosity had got the better of her and also she defended her decision by saying she had promised Ingrid she would see it through. She didn't get up at the next break and while looking at the screen she wasn't really aware what was on it. She was mystified and puzzled at the man's strange behaviours. But while the answer seemed simple, the whole thing was obviously not as simple as it appeared. It had to do with Saskia but the main question kept on coming back: why doesn't he just knock on her door. Alice had a strong urge to phone Saskia to tell her that her old boyfriend was watching from across the road. But she didn't. 'It's not really my business. The only thing I am interested in is getting this woman out of the building.' She nodded and closed her eyes for a moment. Yes, that was most important.

Alice woke with a start and focused back on the screen but what was showing now she didn't recognize. The movie had finished and now she didn't know how it had ended. Annoyed for falling asleep and missing the end Alice turned the TV off and went to the window, hoping he had gone. But he was still there.

Shaking her head she looked at her watch and noted the time 16 minutes past eleven. For goodness sake, go home man and let me go to bed. This is too ridiculous for words. She was getting angry now at what she thought was stupid and infantile behaviour by a grown man who obviously didn't have the guts to face whatever it was, square on.

Alice lowered the binoculars, angry, frustrated, sorry now she promised Ingrid she'd see it through, when suddenly wide awake and interested: "Hallo, what is that?!" Alice said, half aloud, instantly wide awake. 'He's getting out of his car and locking it. For goodness sake he's coming across. He's going to see her. Halleluya! I've got to phone Ingrid. "Sorry if I have woken you up Ingrid, but the man has just crossed the road. I'm sure he's going to see her."

"Thanks Alice. I'll go and see what's happening. Talk to you later, bye."

Hoping she hadn't missed him, Alice ran to the stairs and down to the fourth floor. Peering through the slightly ajar door she was just in time to see the businessman force his way in. The urge to go and listen at the door was very strong but realizing it to be too risky; Alice stayed in the stairwell waiting to see what would happen next. Sooner or later and hopefully sooner, he'll come out again, because I think it's not going to be a friendly call.

CHAPTER 21

Alan had gone to see Emma in the afternoon. But instead of going home and cooking himself dinner as he had promised, Alan, after a quick meal in a restaurant; again found a spot from where he could see the entrance to the apartments. Since Saskia didn't want to talk to him; Alan had decided not to give her a choice. He'd make her talk to him.

It was not only the letters now, but talking to Emma as well. But of course he had to be certain she was in and alone. Alan was getting desperate. It was now Friday and so far he hadn't had any luck. She always had men around her. Alan paused at the thought, then it dawned on him; 'she's a bloody prostitute. That's what she is. I've been fucking a bloody prostitute.' Alan shuddered at the thought. It was hard to believe but everything pointed to it. A different man every evening and Gods knows what she did during the day. 'Boy, you're a bit bloody slow to wake up to this only now,' he did mutter to himself: 'So that's how she made a living?' He had always thought she had independent means and didn't need to work. 'But why,' he wondered, 'has she never asked me, or even hinted at, that she wanted to be paid, as it was obvious it was her livelihood?'

Strange. Alan shook his head, still finding it difficult to accept. She was such a lady, she was beautiful, she had poise. But just imagine moving in with her as she had suggested? Alan allowed himself a chuckle. He'd finish up a bloody pimp.

Every evening he had been watching she had been with a man and now it was Friday. Alan hadn't seen anybody he'd associate with Saskia going in or coming out and just as he was about to go and see her, Saskia came out with a man he had not seen going in.

Alan looked at his watch, just after 7.

The well-dressed man, like all the other men he had seen with Saskia, said something and Saskia laughed heartedly. 'The bloody bitch,' Alan fumed, 'there she was laughing and joking while making his and Emma's life a misery.' He shook his head despairingly. 'The bitch had kept this part of her life well hidden.' A taxi pulled up and they got in.

'What the bloody hell now.' Upset and angry, Alan thumped the top of the car. 'How the bloody hell can I even get to her with all these men hanging around and it doesn't look like she is suffering too much either? Alan got back in the car. 'Go home! Alan shrugged. 'They'd obviously gone to dinner.' Something else she had never suggested and just as well. He wouldn't have been too happy about it. 'Anyway I'm sure they'll finish up in bed when they come back. Go home!' Alan shrugged. 'Bloody prostitute. Move in with her? God help me. He ought to bloody well wring her bloody neck when, or if rather, he finally got to see her. Maybe,' Alan guffawed, 'she's trying it on now with one of the other fellows.'

A taxi pulled up and Saskia and the man got out. The man was carrying a full plastic bag. 'They bloody well got a take away' Alan mumbled incredulously, as he watched the two disappear inside.

'Now what? Go home.' He shook his head, if he'd go every time there was a bloke involved, he'd never get to see her. But of course there is this possibility, and I should have thought about that before, like me, the fellow may have to go home to his wife.

'No, I'll stay at least till eleven, or maybe till half past eleven.'

Finding himself dozing off, Alan switched on the radio forcing himself to listen to talk and music. Watching the time moving ever so slowly Alan cursed the man for not leaving and Saskia for putting him in this situation. Eleven o'clock came and went. 10 minutes past, 11 minutes past – Alan had begun to count the minutes at 15 minutes past. Alan, sighing deeply dejected by shaking his head. 'Another wasted evening. What on earth am I going to do? I can't keep doing this. Tomorrow night I'm going in. Too it. Too bad if she's got somebody there. For goodness sake, she's got to take some time off work. OK then. Tomorrow night. Straightening up from his slouched position; Alan started the car and was about to put the lever into drive, when the front door opened and the man came out. Almost at the same time a large car pulled up and the man got in.

'Well bugger that,' Alan uttered, completely taken by surprise. 'This probably has been happening other evenings as well.' He switched off the engine, got out of his car, locked it and quickly walked across to the front entrance to the building. Once inside Alan paused: 'Lift or stairs? Lift' he decided. Once on the fourth floor and standing in front of Saskia's apartment he realized that now came the difficult part. How to get inside.

Announcing himself wouldn't do any good. Seeing she had told him categorically she didn't want to see him anymore. Cursing under his breath for not working this out before, barging in, Alan pressed the bell. All he could really do was to make Saskia believe the bloke had come back.

Nothing happened for what seemed a long time. Getting impatient and angry he pressed the bell again. Wondering what he would do if she didn't open the door. 'What the bloody hell could he do? Belt down the door?' Alan was beginning to panic; standing in front of her door visibly agitated if someone would happen to come. He doubted she was asleep. Most likely standing behind the door, apprehensively wondering who it was and what to do. Alan was about to press the bell again when he heard a small worried voice: "Who is there?" Is that you Vince?"

Hand in front of his mouth Alan whispered, "Yes, it's me."

Another few agonizing long moments and Alan heard the bolt sliding back and the key turning in the lock. As the door opened Alan immediately pushed hard against it, sending Saskia sprawling on her back. Once inside Alan slammed the door shut behind him.

Stunned at the sudden attack, Saskia, in negligee, stared up at her attacker, petrified, then when she recognised who it was, scrambled to her feet, shouting angrily, hysterically: "Get out, get out you bastard or I'll call the police."

Staring furiously at Saskia in the dim light of the entrance, Alan said: "I phoned to ask you for us to meet somewhere, but since you refused I'm doing it this way. Now, what's got into you? First sending me these stupid letters and now upsetting my wife. Now, all I want you to do is to tell me that you are going to stop bothering us. Do I make myself clear?!"

"Get out, get out, Saskia was shouting, furiously, verging on hysteria. "Who the hell do you think you are forcing yourself in here and telling me what to do? How dare you. Get out you bastard. I don't want to have anything to do with you. But I will tell your wife what we've been doing, if she hasn't already guessed something has been going on."

"Yes. You've given her enough clues, but I'm warning you and don't play the hurt and innocent girl with me. You're a prostitute, a whore. I've been watching you and you don't seem too sad and hurt to me. Tell me, how are the other fellows doing?" Alan added sarcastically, "Are you blackmailing them too? Do you want money to shut you up? Is that your game?"

"Get out, get out," Saskia was now screaming hysterically, while trying to push Alan towards the front door. Grabbing hold of Saskia, Alan pushed her into the living room shouting: "Shut up, you stupid bitch. You're mad. You're bloody insane. What made you think there was anything between us? You're a slut, sleeping around until you find a sucker stupid enough to stay with you."

Beside herself with anger at his insults, Saskia lashed out and hit Alan in his face with all the power she could muster while screaming: "Get out, get out, you filthy bastard."

Momentarily taken aback by the ferociousness of the blow, Alan blinked and shook his head.

Still screaming: "Get out, get out," Saskia is now hitting Alan wherever she could with both fists. But unlike the first blow, they were not hurting him.

To stop her Alan suddenly hit Saskia hard in her face, splitting her lips. Saskia stopped and drew back and staring at Alan, hissed with all the venom she could muster: "I'm going to tell your wife and you can't stop me and I'll also show her what you are doing to me now."

Incensed at Saskia's taunt, Alan hit her again, hard, full in the face, shouting: "Don't even well fucking think of it. I'll kill you if you do."

The hit to her face had made Saskia step back. She could feel the swelling coming up and a trickle of warm liquid filled her lips. Now silently crying in frustration but defiant, Saskia looked at Alan, the only man she had ever loved and had loved with such intensity, it had frightened her. At the same time it had given her joy and contentment. Now her dreams and the promise of a life together in love with someone and being loved in return had been shattered. Now she hated him, hated him with the same intensity as she had loved him.

"I am going to tell your wife," Saskia said, much calmer now, "and I will tell her everything. And if you are going to kill me because of that you might as well kill me now. But I know now. You're a coward, a miserable weak little caricature of a man and you're not doing anything. You haven't got the guts. Now, get out or I'll call the police."

For a few moments Alan stared at Saskia, not believing what he had just heard. 'This woman, this bloody whore was now insulting and mocking him and still going to tell Emma. Then with a howl he threw himself at Saskia, savagely punching her in the face and chest. Stumbling backward under the ferocity of the blows, Saskia lost her balance and on falling down hit her head against the edge of the low coffee table in the centre of the room, knocking her unconscious.

His chest heaving, Alan looked at the now inert body at his feet, then it hit him: "Oh my God, I've killed her," and a jolt of fear and panic surged through him. He knelt beside her: 'Don't die Saskia, please don't die, please. I'm sorry. I didn't mean to hit you so hard.'

Bending over her he looked at her closely. She was still breathing, he was sure. He felt her pulse. At first he couldn't feel any and a renewed surge of panic went through him. Then he felt it, faint, but it was there. 'Yes, there was a pulse. She wasn't dead.'

Relieved he got up off the floor and looked down at Saskia. He couldn't believe what he had just done. He had never hit anyone, let alone a woman. Troubled, he didn't know what to do. She needed help. She could still die if she didn't get it. Alan felt the perspiration of fear and indecision soaking his clothes.

'I didn't mean to hit you," Alan said to the still body on the floor, 'but you made me so angry. Why don't you just forget about it, us? There is no future in it. I made that clear.' Alan walked a few steps towards the door, stopped and turned around. Troubled, worried, he looked at Saskia, still lying there not moving. He should ring for an ambulance. But then, he reminded himself he may have to explain how and why he came to be here and how she got in this condition. And one thing would lead to another. He shook his head sadly. He couldn't do that. They also could find out who called, even if he got out before they came. He couldn't afford the scandal. She was alive and she was a strong woman.

At the front door Alan paused and peered out into the dimly lit hall. He was sure nobody had seen him go in but now he had to get out without being seen. The lift was still there. Although it was late, it was Friday night and there would still be people about. He pulled the door behind but didn't shut it, in case there was no lift and he had to go back inside again. His lip started to get sore and he ran his tongue over it. It felt like it was split. 'Bloody woman.' He hadn't seen it coming. She packed quite a punch. He pressed the button, the doors opened and Alan hurried inside. After a few anxious moments the doors opened to an empty foyer. He crossed it quickly and almost ran to his car.

As he sat down Alan took a deep breath. It felt as if it was the first breath he had taken since he walked up to the entrance of the building. The relief was immense. He felt light-headed.

As he put the key in the ignition he thought about Saskia lying there. It had not been the way he had wanted to do it but she had left him no choice. If she only had agreed to talk it through, nothing of this would have happened. Also, Alan was upset that he had to leave her in

95

the condition she was in no matter how angry he was with her. If the stupid woman only had listened to reason. But no, she kept on provoking him.

On the way home he began to have doubts again about her being alive. Had he really seen her breathing or felt her pulse ticking? He had wanted that to be, but he had also wanted to get out of there. He probably should have called the ambulance and he should have made more certain that she really was alive. She had to be alive, even if that meant she would go to the police. Suddenly he couldn't care about that anymore. He was no murderer. Oh God, what a mess he had gotten himself into. He should have let her go to Emma and tell all. In fact he himself should have told Emma what had been happening. Emma would have forgiven him. She loved him. Too late for all that now.

Almost home Alan suddenly remembered that in his haste to leave; he had forgotten to pull the door shut..

When Alice saw the businessman going into the lift she got up to go back to her apartment. But then she noticed he hadn't shut the front door. Alice hesitated. Maybe she should wait to see if the woman came to close it because if she didn't she had better go in to see what had happened in there. While she waited she saw Ingrid coming out of her apartment going into the woman's apartment and closing the door behind her.

Alice was relieved to see Ingrid going in which absolved her. But why, she wondered, did she close the door behind her?

After waiting a few more moments, Alice turned around and went back to her apartment telling herself: 'Well, it's now not my problem anymore. And I don't want to be in there with her anyway, telling me, do this and do that.'

Ingrid had become quite bossy lately. For some time now it had become apparent to Alice that Ingrid was used to have people work for her and was used to giving orders. And occasionally Ingrid seemed to have forgotten that they were supposed to be friends and that she, Alice, was not the hired help. Having had to follow orders all her working life and now finally a lady of leisure and equal to everybody else, Alice had begun to resent Ingrid's behaviour.

It sometimes even went as far as looking disapprovingly at the clothes Alice wore. Yes, they were old and not high fashion but they were clean and practical. Right from the beginning Alice had her misgivings about this relationship and she should have listened to her inner voice. A society lady and a working class woman do not mix she had always been told and believed it. Their worlds were different. Maybe this was silly and she was over-sensitive about it but because of Ingrid's behaviour of late; it had been on her mind a lot. She felt she had been let down by the person she thought was her friend. It had been building up slowly, the resentment Alice had begun to feel about this rich and refined woman who played golf, bridge and tennis and told her about her travels in Europe and America, visiting opera houses and art galleries. All the things Alice had never been able to do.

On top of that Alice had begun to resent deeply what she thought, especially lately, was a patronizing attitude Ingrid had adopted towards her. And Alice had convinced herself that Ingrid did this to show her superiority. Ingrid was high society, a class of people Alice, through her birth and upbringing, had always had contempt for. In a way it irked her that now she was hobnobbing with a member of that class. She still could not quite understand why she had agreed to go along with Ingrid's proposal. However, thinking about it again and looking at it in the context of two women by themselves doing things together, it had been, at the time, a reasonable proposal.

CHAPTER 22

After coming home Alan went straight to bed. But, even though physically and mentally exhausted after the confrontation with Saskia, he was unable to go to sleep. The image of Saskia lying on the floor, bleeding, her face bruised and swollen, was playing on his mind. Was she dead or alive? Had he taken enough time to make sure she was alive? He should have phoned for an ambulance. For goodness sake man, he admonished himself a life was at stake here. But, and he considered his next thought slowly. He would have been in terrible trouble. His life, you know, his life, his marriage and his job, all that would have been lost, gone; all his hard work for nothing. He, the respectful businessman, against the life of a common prostitute. No, he decided after some more soul searching, he had taken the right decision. Anyway, she was alive, he knew she was alive. He had felt her pulse and he had definitely detected breathing. She'd be alright. He was sure. All he should really worry about was that she might go to the police. And that was a totally different situation. He would easily be able to defend that.

And it was probably not the first time she had been beaten up by a customer and she might not do anything about it. But he had been a bloody fool to have let it go this far without checking her out. It all had been too easy. Meeting him at the conference, wonder how she got there, taking her back to her apartment and practically straight to bed. 'I should have bloody well woken up then, he chided himself. Anyway I hope she's got the message this time. But I am really sorry for the way I had to make her understand.' Finally Alan reassured himself that everything would be alright and he had really nothing to worry about. He began to relax and fell into a deep sleep which lasted well into the morning.

When he finally woke up he lay quite still, last night's happening slowly coming back. He didn't feel bad about it now, having justified his actions and with that absolving himself of all wrongdoing. It felt sore around his mouth and he touched his lip. The bloody bitch packed quite a wallop. Something else she had probably trained for, defending herself.

He had to admit though, she looked fantastic, a real lady. Everything spot on, including her address. Alan turned his head to look at the bedside clock and was surprised to see it was nearly a quarter to nine. As he got out of bed he noticed blood on the pillowcase. Bloody lip, he should have put a plaster on it.

After a shower and breakfast of coffee and toast; Alan went to his study and switched the computer on, intending to catch up on some work. The picture on the computer was a photo of a gorge at Kakadu National Park. Taken now almost 3 years ago. They always enjoyed looking at it, reminding them of a beautiful and happy holiday.

About an hour later Alan closed down the computer and leaned back in his chair. Sighing, he thought he really should go and see Emma, except he wasn't in the mood to be subjected again to more questions about that lady that had accidently strayed into Emma's room.

Accidentally, my foot, he thought. The bloody bitch knew very well who was in that room. Anyway, this should all be behind them now. Alan got up and even though he was reluctant to go; he got dressed to see Emma and no doubt be subjected to more questions about that lady. Alan sighed. He wouldn't admit it but he was still worried about leaving Saskia lying on the floor like that. Yes, he had checked her pulse but now he wasn't even certain anymore that there had even been a pulse. He had wanted there to be a pulse. His stomach knotted at the next thought. She could have died of shock after the beating he had given her. He shook his head, no, she was alive, she had to be alive. He left her alive. He tried to be positive but not succeeding. But by the time he got in his car he was sure she was alive – or was she?

"Hello, my darling, Alan called out cheerfully.

Almost bouncing into Emma's room, feigning enthusiasm, "How are you?"

Emma smiled, "Gee you are pretty lively. And yes, I'm fine. I really feel good. I am psyching myself up to go home. But what happened to your face, I mean your lip?"

Alan shrugged. "Just being stupid. I dropped something and I went to pick it up, I hit my lip on the bottom drawer of my desk. I hadn't closed it properly. Don't worry about it. It was painful when it happened though."

Emma shook her head. "Silly man. Anyway how is the garden?"

"The garden is looking good. You'll be surprised when you see it. Well, at least I haven't killed anything yet."

As he said it; a picture of Saskia lying lifeless on the floor flashed through his mind, his body stiffened and he visually paled.

Emma stared at him and called out, worriedly: "Alan, what's the matter, what happened?"

Recovering Alan answered: "It's nothing, really. I've had this pain in my shoulder for some time now. I obviously strained it picking up something and sometimes when I move it hurts. Sometimes the pain is pretty severe, like now. I'm looking after it, you know, hot packs. It'll be alright. Don't worry about it. Anyway, what I wanted to say was that the garden is waiting for the green thumb expert to come home and look after it."

Emma smiled: "Won't be long now."

"Oh, I almost forgot. I ran into Harry and Sophie the other day and they sent their best wishes. And Keith and Clare have left for Adelaide to be there for the birth of their first grandchild. And they'll be telling you all about it when they're back. Anyway, my darling, I'll be off now but I'll be back tomorrow. Is there anything you need? You've got plenty of reading I see. Bye now," Alan bent down to kiss her, "love you."

'You've got to take a hold of yourself man' he told himself, walking back to his car. 'You just have to hope that she believed you. But then again, there is no reason for her not to believe me. Oh God, let all this end and let her be alive.' At least she hadn't mentioned Saskia.

CHAPTER 23

Saskia opened her eyes. For a few moments she wondered what she was doing lying on the floor in the lounge-room. Then it all came back to her. How Alan had tricked her to open the door, the shouting, the hitting – she hoped he had gone. Saskia lifted her head to look around but, with a grimace of pain, eased her head back onto the floor. She closed her eyes again but a few moments later Saskia, badly shaken and sore, found the strength to get up. Feeling dizzy she steadied herself as she made her way to the bathroom. Her head was hurting terribly and when she looked in the mirror; she got a shock to see her swollen and bruised face caked with congealed blood from her nose and lip. She wet a hand towel and wiped her face clean. Suddenly it was all too much.

Disillusioned, battered into submission, her hope destroyed Saskia started to cry, sobbing silently at the betrayal of the first and only man she had ever loved. But she would tell his wife, tell all and show her what he had done to silence her. She would not be silenced. Still sobbing Saskia splashed her face with cold water hoping to relieve some of the pain.

Face dripping and eyes closed, Saskia half turned to take the towel off the rack and after dabbing her face dry she looked in the mirror to look at the bruises and as she did she saw her neighbour, the woman who treated her with utter disdain and whose attitude towards her was sheer nastiness; the woman who, for a reason Saskia was at a loss to understand, was always rude, sometimes even hostile when they happened to cross paths. That woman was now standing right behind her, angry, menacing. Saskia froze.

It took several long moments before she had recovered enough to turn around. As she did and before she had even time to ask Ingrid what she thought she was doing in her apartment, Ingrid had already put her hands around Saskia's throat.

At first too stunned to move Saskia stared wide eyed into Ingrid's eyes reflecting only intense hatred.

Suddenly, as if only now Saskia realized that the woman was going to kill her she tried, gasping and wheezing to prize the woman's hands away from her throat.

But Saskia, already weakened by the battering from Alan, was no match for Ingrid whose hatred and revulsion of Saskia's chosen life held her throat in a vice like grip.

"Die, die, die, you dirty whore," Ingrid hissed in Saskia's face, beside herself with rage, "die, die, die." They were the last words Saskia heard, eyes glazing over.

Suddenly Saskia slumped to the floor. Keeping her hands tightly around Saskia's throat for a few more moments to make sure she was dead, Ingrid finally straightened up.

While staring coldly at the body at her feet, Ingrid suddenly felt strangely empty and lightheaded. It was as if the emotions of hate and revulsion of what had driven her to do this had melted away with the death of Saskia and she felt that now, with Saskia's death, a chapter in her life that had been festering in the back of her mind up to now, had been brought to a close. The anti-climax was unsettling and suddenly Ingrid felt exhausted, almost dizzy, as she shuffled a few steps backwards, her eyes still on Saskia, before turning around and leaving the bathroom.

By the time she had arrived at the front door Ingrid had recovered. At the door she made sure there was nobody around and pulling the door shut behind her quickly went into her apartment. Once inside Ingrid stood for a few moments before making her way to the lounge-room. The main light was on and she switched it off, leaving one small light on the cabinet. She looked at her hands and it was as if she only now realized what she had done. She had never wanted to do this but her hate had made her lose all perspective and she had done it. She had gone into Saskia's apartment with only one thought in mind: to kill the whore. The hate was revulsion that had made her do this again and had been lying dormant all those years, almost removed from her mind, but it had come back when she first learned of Saskia's profession and it had been playing on her mind ever since. Again she looked at her hands and instantly ran to the bathroom squirting blobs of soap onto her hands and kept washing and scrubbing them, as if it was possible to rub away the pressure with which she had killed Saskia.

Memories flooded back. Then too, when coming home she had washed and scrubbed her hands, as if, this was going to absolve her from taking a young woman's life. It was several minutes before Ingrid finally turned off the tap and dried her hands but even then she could still feel Saskia's skin on her hands. Unable to relax Ingrid went back to the lounge-room and sat down. She tried not to think about what she had just done. But whatever else she tried to think of, choking Saskia to death always came back.

But then, imperceptibly, from having qualms and feeling terrible, Ingrid began to tell herself that what she had done had been the right thing to do. 'No,' she said suddenly and obstinately shaking her head: 'I am not sorry.' Of course sooner or later the body would be discovered and no doubt the police would come asking questions. She would tell them about the businessman, about the shouting and how it suddenly had gone quiet. Ingrid nodded, 'Yes, that's what she would tell the police.'

She was certain she had not left any clues to say that she had been inside.

It was only later in bed and almost asleep when she remembered pulling the front door shut. It made her lie away and worry the rest of the night, thinking. How she was going to explain her finger prints on the inside of the front door.

CHAPTER 24

"That bloody TV was loud last night," Hugo Weller said to his wife, Marcia at breakfast. "Some people just don't consider their neighbours."

"That wasn't TV," Marcia said. "That was people having a terrible argument."

"I reckon it was TV," Hugo insisted.

"And I think it came from the apartment above us," Marcia continued, ignoring Hugo. "I wonder what went on in there and why? She is such a nice person, a real lady. Always gives you the time of day."

When Hugo, more interested in his newspaper didn't answer, Marcia too, turned to her part from the paper.

After a leisurely breakfast and cleaning up Marcia looked at the wall clock. 10 minutes to 9. She was unsettled. She couldn't shake the feeling that something awful had happened. It had not just been a normal bit of shouting. They wouldn't even hear that. People in the building were considerate.

"Hugo?"

"Yes, what?"

"Do you think you should go and see if she's alright?"

"It's got nothing to do with us. If people want to get into an argument that's their business. I'm sure she's alright. I don't want us to get involved."

"Who says we're getting involved? All you're going to do is find out if she's alright. And if you don't....."

"OK. OK. I'll go and see her."

A little later Hugo is back: "She's not answering her door. Maybe she's gone out. But her newspaper is still at the door and that is a bit odd."

"Oh, I don't like that" Marcia said, "Maybe we should go to the police."

"Look, I've done what you asked me to do and that's the end of it, OK?" Hugo said, getting cross.

"Now, Hugo," Marcia answered conciliatory, "You said yourself that's odd to have the newspaper still at the front door at this time of the morning. Maybe she's hurt and lying there helpless, or maybe she's dying. We've got to do something. Let's tell Glenda then, and if you're not going to do that, I will," Marcia added determinately.

"Oh, alright, alright," Hugo held up his hand. "OK, but I don't want to have any more to do with it after this."

"Glenda?" Hugo said when the manager answered the phone, "The wife is a bit concerned about the woman who lives in the apartment above us. She says there was a terrible argument there last night. I thought it was the TV. Anyway this morning the wife insisted I go and find out how she is but she's not answering her door and the newspaper is still outside. And I must admit that's a bit odd."

"Yes," Glenda agreed, "Yes, that is unusual, but maybe she is sleeping in. Let's give it a bit more time, say, another hour and then I'll go and have a look."

"Another hour, yeah that's OK, see you – oh, hang on Glenda, the wife wants to say something."

"Glenda, Marcia speaking, look Glenda, there was a terrible and I mean really terrible row in the apartment above us last night. God knows what happened, but I think we should go and have a look now. And if you don't I'll call the police. The woman may be badly hurt and needs medical attention."

There was a short silence, then: "OK I'll come up. But are you sure she's home? Have you tried to phone her?"

"We don't have her number and anyway if she's badly hurt she won't be able to come to the phone."

"OK. I'll come up now. But I would like you to be there too."

"We'll be there."

"I told you I don't want us to get involved," Hugo said. "It's got nothing to do with us."

"Don't you worry," Marcia said, walking to the front door. "I'll go by myself. We can't let the poor woman lying there injured without any help."

"Oh, for God's sake," Hugo said emphatically, annoyed at his wife's stubbornness, "next you'll have her dead."

Stepping out of the lift and walking towards Hugo and Marcia, Glenda said: "Now, if she's got the bolt on, presuming she is home, we won't be able to get in unless we break the door down. And I'm not going to do that. But if you still want to keep going with it we'll have to get the police. Oh – er – by the way, I phoned but her answering machine is on. OK then, here goes" Having selected a key Glenda put it in the lock, a turn, a push and the door opened.

Expecting the door to be bolted, Glenda frowned and looking at Hugo and Marcia said: "That's not right, she should have bolted the door. And it's not even on the deadlock. I don't know now. Maybe we should get the police."

"Yes, OK. Go get them. But I'm going in," Marcia said determinedly, "She may be lying in badly injured and she needs help now. If we wait for the police she could be dead by the time they arrive."

Glenda nodded: "Yes. OK then. Let's go in calling out. Saskia, hallo, Saskia where are you."

"I don't like this, Marcia said, pointing to an upturned chair in the lounge-room, "I'm sure something has happened to her," and went to put the chair right.

"Don't touch it" Glenda shouted, then apologized. "Sorry for shouting but until we know what has been going on here we had better leave things as they are. Let's have a look in the bedroom."

Glenda led the way into the bedroom and turning into the ensuite, they saw the body, still in a slumped position on the floor against the wall.

Shocked and speechless they stared at the body, then regaining composure Glenda quickly ushered the others out. But back in the lounge-room Glenda hesitated and, wondering if she was really dead, turned back wanting to make sure. Nervously she approached the body and when she touched Saskia's neck to feel a pulse she withdrew her hand as if stung. The body was ice cold, fanning the others in the lounge-room she said: "I had better call the police."

"I told you," Marcia said tearfully, dabbing her eyes with a tissue, "that something dreadful had happened to her. I just knew it."

"Don't go too far away," Glenda said, "The cops might want to talk to you."

"I want you to leave us out of this Glenda" Hugo said, "I don't want us to get involved." And turning to Marcia he added: "I told you to stay out of it. It's got nothing to do with us, and now we are involved. We don't even know the woman."

"Oh, shut up, Hugo," Marcia said, still upset and sniveling, getting angry now at her husband's whinging.

Ignoring them, Glenda closed the front door and said: "I'll go down and call the cops."

Back in this apartment Hugo, angry, told Marcia "Don't tell me to shut up in front of hired hands."

"Then stop whinging about not wanting to get involved. For God's sake Hugo, a human being has just been murdered. And all we'll do is just tell the police what we know and that isn't much."

CHAPTER 25

Uniformed police arrived within 10 minutes, assessed the situation, set up a crime scene and called in detectives from Sydney City.

"I'm afraid I can't tell you much," Glenda said to the detective in charge, Sergeant Sam Horwell, "it's the people who live just below this apartment who persuaded me to have a look. They were worried something had happened to the lady who lives here.

"Apparently there was some yelling and screaming. And that's all I can tell you. Do you mind if I go now? I'll be in my office if you need me."

Sam Horwell nodded. "Yeah, OK," and turning to Detective Senior Constable Peter Menkin, he suggested, "Let's go down to the people who heard the noise."

"I've been expecting you," Marcia said, "please come in."

After the detectives had introduced themselves, Marcia said: "Would you like a cup of coffee?"

"No, thank you. This won't take long. The manager told us that you were worried something had happened to the occupant of the apartment above you. What gave you that idea?"

"Well, I – er we heard shouting and screaming. It was terrible, really scary. We had been thinking of getting the police but it was a bit difficult to determine where it came from at first. And when we finally decided it came from the apartment above us, it had stopped. Also my husband was sure it was on the TV."

"And why did you think it came from the apartment above you?"

"Well, Marcia said with a glance at Hugo, "there is a lady living there all by herself."

"Is that a reason to think the screaming came from there?"

"Well, er –" Marcia again glanced at Hugo, trying to involve him, but Hugo studiously avoided eye contact.

Annoyed at Hugo for not helping her, Marcia continued, "We think she had men friends."

"Men friends?" Sam Horwell raised his eyebrows.

"Er – well, yes. Men friends, er –" Marcia hesitated, not wanting to pass judgment. "Er– well er – she entertained men – I think."

"You mean she was a prostitute?" Detective Horwell put it bluntly.

"Oh no," Marcia recoiled, shocked at the suggestion. "No, I didn't mean that at all. We wouldn't have anybody like that in the building. Oh no," Marcia shook her head sternly, "she is a nice woman."

"But she had men friends."

"Yes," Hugo suddenly taking an interest, chipped in. "I've seen them, men, coming and going."

"That's not true," Marcia said, looking accusingly at Hugo, "and anyway, that doesn't mean anything. She is a single woman and entitled to have men friends."

"What time do you think this was happening?"

"Oh, it must have been around 11.30. We had been looking at a movie and that finished around 20 past 11."

Sam Horwell nodded: "Thank you very much. You've been very helpful. If you think of anything else, anything at all, please give us a call. There is my card."

"We don't want to be involved," Hugo said as he let the detectives out, "It's got nothing to do with us."

"Thank you very much, sir. Goodbye," Sam Horwell said politely, ignoring Hugo's last effort at not to get involved.

"Let's have a chat with the people living next door to the deceased," Sam said to Peter Menkin, "and find out what they can tell us."

"Good morning Madam. Sorry to disturb you. I am Detective Sergeant Sam Horwell and this is Detective Senior Constable Peter Menkin. I wonder if we could ask you a few questions about your neighbour?"

"Yes of course. Please come in."

"What's going on, what's happened?" Ingrid said as she led the detectives into the lounge-room. "I saw you talking to the manager earlier on."

"The lady in that apartment is deceased, and we are wondering if you heard or saw anything last night, and if you did about what time?"

"Well, there was a lot of shouting and screaming at one stage. I don't know the exact time but it was after eleven. I had been looking at a movie and had trouble going to sleep. It was then that I heard it and then suddenly all was quiet."

"How well did you know her?" Detective Horwell asked. "Oh, not very well. She kept to herself."

"Did she have friends. I mean, did you notice people coming and going?"

"Yes, there were people visiting her and from what I saw they were mainly men. But I didn't take all that much notice. I mean I wasn't spying on her."

"I'm not suggesting that."

"There was a period though," Ingrid said, quasi pensively. "That I think she must have had a steady boyfriend and, at that time, he was the only one to come around. But something must have happened and she went back to her old ways."

"What do you mean by 'her old ways'?"

Ingrid looked pained: "Well, I don't want to say anything bad about her, but, er – well, I think she was a professional, you know, an escort if you know what I mean?"

"It must be difficult for you to tell us these things about your neighbour, but if we want to find out who did this, we have to know about her personal life."

Ingrid nodded, thoughtfully, "Um – this is probably of interest too. I've told you about the, what I called, the boyfriend. Well, I've been coming home a few evenings after 7 o'clock and I noticed this man who I presumed was her boyfriend watching the building from across the road. I wondered then what he was doing. I mean, if he wanted to talk to her when not just come across and ring the bell."

"This – er – boyfriend, what does he look like? I mean, is he old, young, big, tall?"

"Oh. I'd say he's around the fifties, tallish, good-looking, light brown hair, a bit greying at the temples. Always well dressed. You know, suit and tie. He looked like a businessman."

"Do you happen to know his name?"

"No, but I thought of a possible reason he was watching the building. He could have found out about her activities and was angry about it. He then watched and waited until she was alone and gave her a good belting."

Senior Constable Menkin made a note in his notebook: 'In her words: he then watched and waited until she was alone and gave her a good belting. She did NOT say waited until she was alone and killed her.'

Detective Sergeant Horwell stood up: "That's it for now Mrs?"

"It's Ms Freeman. I'm a widow," Ingrid finished his question. "And I live alone."

"Thank you for your time. You have been very helpful."

"Letting them out Ingrid said: "Yes, I hope I have been of some help. I really didn't have much to do with her, apart from the usual pleasantries. She seemed a nice person."

Walking across to Saskia's apartment, Menkin said: "Mrs Freeman said, and I quote 'she had been belted up and NOT she had been killed.'"

"Yes, interesting, isn't it?" Horwell answered.

Back in Saskia's apartment one of the forensic officers of the team spoke to Sergeant Horwell: "We've found the woman's diary. It makes for interesting reading."

CHAPTER 26

Watching the evening news on TV while eating his pizza and sipping a glass of red, Alan suddenly gagged on his pizza and a jab of anxiety hit his stomach, when he heard the newsreader say, 'A woman has been found dead in her apartment in Park Street in the City. The police are treating it as a murder."

When he finally got over the shock he told himself that this could not be Saskia, because when he left she was alive. He had made sure of that. He tried to put his mind at ease by telling himself that there was more than one apartment building in Park Street but the uneasy feeling remained. His appetite gone he threw the rest of the pizza in the bin, finished his glass of red and sat down. Worriedly he wondered what could have happened after he had left. After all, he had left the front door open.

CHAPTER 27

Mrs Miller took the plastic away from her Sunday newspaper and spread it out on the table. She liked to read the paper while having her breakfast. On the top in the centre column was a photo of a woman's head. Frowning Mrs Miller stared at it. The woman looked vaguely familiar. She read the caption. 'Murdered. Late Friday night or early Saturday morning this woman was murdered in the bathroom of her apartment. Anyone with information on anybody acting suspicious at that time are asked to contact Police.

Mrs Miller looked again at the photo. It was a beautiful face and in death a serene calmness emanated from it. So this was the woman mentioned on the TV last night? Mrs Miller kept looking, willing her brain to remember, saying: 'I know you. I've met you somewhere.' She suddenly remembered, of course, that was her. The lovely lady who had come to the front door of the Henderson's residence and had handed her a letter for Mr Henderson, asking her to put it where he would see it. She had put it on his desk, knowing that that was where he would go to.

Mrs Miller nodded. 'Yes, that was her. Poor woman. Such a lovely lady. Who would want to kill her? Mr and Mrs Henderson must be terribly upset. It's obviously somebody they know very well. I must say something about it to Mr Henderson.'

CHAPTER 28

Emma was doing well. She felt herself getting stronger almost daily. The nurse taking her blood pressure and temperature had just left and Emma closed her eyes again. It wouldn't be long now. Going home! She mouthed the words. She was often thinking about that and wondering how her home looked with somebody else doing the housework. It would certainly make it easier on Alan. He had been really good coming almost every day and some days even twice. The last visits had been somewhat strained but that had been because of that woman. It was as if she really knew Alan and although he denied knowing her, Emma did not quite believe him. Like Emma didn't believe anymore that the woman coming into her room had been accidental. And certainly not after her second visit. Emma had talked to Marjorie about it but even she could not put her mind at ease. All Marjorie could say in the end was that the Alan she knew Alan would not do anything like that and if you really think that that is what is going on is true, he must have had a complete behaviour makeover.

'Well, anyway,' Emma decided, 'when she turns up again I'm not going to let here leave without telling me how she knows Alan and what their relationship is. Neither of them had been honest with her,' she felt. But this time she would demand some answers from both of them.

A cheery, "Good morning, Mrs H, here's your brekkie," interrupted Emma's thoughts. Seeing the food Emma was suddenly hungry. There had been times when she couldn't even look at food, let along eat it. Emma had just pulled the lid off the orange juice, took a sip and while pouring the milk on her cereal, the lady selling newspapers walked in. Pulling the paper closer the first thing she saw was a photo of the woman she knew as Sassie, her mysterious visitor. For a few moments Emma stared at the image, transfixed, then she lowered her eyes to read the caption: murdered, she read, late Friday night or early Saturday morning. This woman was murdered in the bathroom of her apartment.

Emma did not read any further. Suddenly her heart started beating faster and her body broke out in a cold sweat and a terrible thought entered her head; a thought she rejected immediately but refused to go away. Her next thought hit even harder. He killed her so she couldn't visit her anymore and give their secret away. Pressing her hands against her chest, to try to stop the loud banging within and gulping air, Emma thought she was going to faint but it passed.

Calming down she shook her head. 'What an earth was I thinking? Of course Alan has nothing to do with it. You were only thinking like that because this woman had come to see you, and Alan's rather clumsy denials that he knew her. Of course he knew the woman. Emma was sure. She had been thinking for some time now that there was something going on between them and that the late meetings had been with this woman and had nothing to do with work. Dejectedly she shook her head. 'God, she had been stupid, naïve and trusting. Of course that this woman had been murdered just now was a coincidence, it had to be.'

But as much as she wanted to believe that, and that Alan had nothing to do with it, Emma could not put out of her mind the thought she had when she first saw the photo, then she thought of his split lip and his strong reaction when he said he hadn't killed anything – her mind lingered on the word anything – anyone – Emma slowly eased back into the pillows and close her eyes. It felt as if she wasn't anymore, but she was.

CHAPTER 29

It was Sunday morning, 8am and Alan stood in front of the mirror in the bathroom. He'd had a shave and a shower and felt better and more relaxed than he had for quite some time. He gingerly touched his lip with a tissue. It had opened up again under the shower and had started to bleed, not much, but enough for it to be an annoyance.

'Bloody woman,' he muttered. 'It happened so fast I just had not seen it coming. Anyway.' he thought, 'if this was all he had to suffer to stop her going to see Emma and writing these stupid letters it was worth it.' Alan nodded at his image in the mirror. 'Right! That's it. Let's what happened be put behind us and concentrate on the future and the first thing is getting Emma out of hospital and our lives back to normal. No more cheating and no more lies..' He touched his lip and suddenly felt guilty, very aware and deeply regretting that the start of their new lives had to begin with a lie.

Alan sighed as he went down to the kitchen to make himself a cup of coffee and have breakfast, thinking 'It is still better Emma doesn't know what really has happened.'

While the water was dripping through the coffee grinds, he went to get his newspaper. Back in the kitchen he put bread in the toaster, poured himself a cup of coffee and while taking the plastic wrapper off the paper he thought: 'I should go to the office, clear up some backlog and then go and see Emma and talk to her about coming home.'

The paper fell open on the front page and the first thing he saw was a photo of Saskia, then his eyes dropped to the caption. 'Murdered,' he read and he got such a shock he had to steady himself against the table as he dropped heavily on a chair. For a moment it was as if his body had shut down. 'I killed her,' he mumbled, his body breaking out in a cold sweat. 'I killed her but I didn't mean to. It was an accident. She fell, Oh my God, I am sorry. I am so sorry. What am I going to do?'

For some time Alan just sat, arms resting on his thighs and in his mind repeating over and over: 'I killed her, I killed her. It was an accident.'

After some time when he had recovered somewhat he read the caption: 'Murdered. Late Friday night or early Saturday morning. This woman was murdered in the bathroom of her apartment.'

Alan couldn't read any further. He felt sick thinking of what was going to happen now. It would be investigated and then they would find out he had been there; but of course not necessarily that particular night. Having calmed down some more he read the caption but stopped at the word 'bathroom'? Alan frowned. 'But that was not where she was when he left her. When he left she was lying on the floor in the lounge-room and she was alive. He had made sure of that. Now, to get up from the floor, go to the bathroom and drop dead there ---?! Alan pulled a face, hard to believe. But the next thought made him break out in a cold sweat again. 'She could have left a note telling the police that I had been there.'

Then it suddenly hit him. 'The front door! He had left it ajar and hadn't shut it so that he could run inside if somebody came while he was waiting for the lift. And in his haste to get away he had forgotten about it. Somebody must have noticed that the door was not shut, gone in and murdered her. That was it of course. But she was on the fourth floor. Would somebody from the street wonder in? An opportunistic burglar maybe, going from floor to floor? Highly unlikely, but possible.

Devastated Alan sat, staring at the photo, every now and then shaking his head, as the enormity of his involvement and the implications of that began to sink in. Emma he knew also got the newspaper and by now would have seen the photo and recognize her as the woman who had visited her and had given her clues about knowing her husband. He had denied knowing her of course but he knew that Emma had not believed him, just giving him the benefit of the doubt.

And what would she be thinking now? Alan felt sick to the stomach as he imagined what she could be thinking. He really should go and tell her he had nothing to do with it. Yes, he knew her and he was sorry for lying about that, but that was where it ended. 'If she only wasn't in that bloody hospital.'

He went back over his encounter with Saskia. 'Would there be anything that could put him in her apartment? Involuntarily he touched his lip – sighing heavily, he murmured 'What have I done?'

Totally immersed in trying to come to terms with the turn of events; Alan was oblivious to anything happening around him but the persistent ringing of the doorbell finally got to him.

Mechanically, his mind still on what he had just seen in the newspaper, and his possible involvement, Alan got up and opened the door to two well-dressed men.

"Mr Henderson? Mr Alan Henderson?"

Alan nodded resignedly. He was not surprised. It was as if he had been expecting them.

"I am Detective Sergeant Horwell and this is Detective Senior Constable Menkin," the spokesman said, both showing their identification. "May we come in please?"

Again Alan nodded, opening the door wider to let them in.

In the lounge-room Alan, dejectedly slumped in a chair, gesturing to the two detectives to also take a seat.

Thanking Alan, and after sitting down, Sergeant Horwell took a photo of Saskia out of his pocket and showed it to Alan: "Do you know this woman?"

Alan nodded.

"How do you know her, Mr Henderson?" The tone was pleasant, conversational. "I mean is she a friend, a business associate or do you visit her for extra marital favours? You have visited her, haven't you, Mr Henderson?"

Again Alan nodded.

"When was the last time you saw her, Mr Henderson?"

The question stirred something in Alan. "I'm sorry," he said, straightening up suddenly alert. "What did you say?"

"I said, Sergeant Horwell repeated, "When was the last time you saw her?"

"I'm sorry, but I'm not answering anymore questions. I would like to talk to my solicitor."

"You were with her in her apartment on Friday night, weren't you Mr Henderson?"

"I want to talk to my solicitor."

"Of course, Mr Henderson. We'll be in touch. And – er- that's a nasty cut in your lip, Mr Henderson. Thank you for your time. We'll let ourselves out."

Alan remained in his chair, thinking and wondering how they had been able to tie him to Saskia, and so quickly. As far as he knew there was nothing that could connect him to her. People may have seen him in the building but nobody – Alan stopped. Of course, the neighbour, she had seen him waiting to go inside. But she didn't know his name, he was sure and describing him still wouldn't get his name. So how – Alan suddenly remembered. The diary! Saskia kept a diary.

His heart sank and a jolt of unease went through him. The bloody diary! She would have written about him. He had seen it one evening lying open on her dresser. She had obviously been writing in it just before he came and he had gone over to have a look.

But she had quickly closed it and smiling embarrassingly had put it in a drawer. He had never seen it again. He should have looked for it and taken it, but he had forgotten about it.

OK so they had seen the diary and his name would have been in it. But so most likely would have been names of men, other men, seeing what she did for a living. But that still didn't connect him with Saskia's murder. That had to be pure speculation.

However he was uneasy about them mentioning the cut in his lip but that could have been just an observation.

Sitting in the chair Alan stared morosely at the floor in front of him contemplating the turn of events. The morning which had started so positive had been shattered. The breakfast he had been looking forward to, forgotten. The problem that had tormented him for so long and had caused him so much grief had not only not been solved but had compounded with a vengeance. Nodding grimly Alan realized the precarious position he was in. He was under suspicion. He was a person of interest. They had made it clear that they knew that he knew her. But of course they still would have to prove that he had been there that Friday night. At that thought he involuntarily touched his lip as it suddenly occurred to him that if his blood was on her fist he was in trouble, serious trouble.

At that thought Alan took his mobile and rang his solicitor. He was not in his office, not home and his mobile was switched off. Upset and angry he couldn't speak with him, Alan left a rather cryptic message to get in touch as soon as possible.

CHAPTER 30

Examining the body closely, the pathologist said: "She did get a heavy blow to the head, as she fell and hit her head on something solid. But that was not the cause of death," and he added with conviction, "the death was caused by strangulation and this was done by a person with small hands. There had been a fight and she was roughed up before she got the heavy blow to the head. Her face is bruised and swollen. Also some skin from the woman's right hand is missing and it has been bleeding. We sent blood that was on her hand to the lab for DNA but it very well could be hers, seeing she cleaned herself up. We've also swabbed her neck for DNA from the offenders hands and sent that off too. But whoever she connected with has a slightly damaged face. She has ointment on her hands to put on the cuts and bruises. It never got there. She was disturbed by the person who was going to kill her."

"So what are you saying?" Sergeant Horwell said, "is that there are two people involved? The person that belted her up and the person that killed her?"

"Yes, and if the person she had the argument with had wanted to kill her, why wait until she goes to the bathroom? I doubt she would have gone to the bathroom and do what she did with that person there." The pathologist shook his head, "No, it is my belief the person who belted her up had left and somehow another person managed to get inside and strangle her. And that is the person with the small hands. We have the result of the fingerprints and apart from the deceased and the manager there are two other sets of prints. Both of these are on the outside and also on the inside of the front door. We have found out that apart from the fingerprints of both the deceased and the manager being present, there are two other sets of prints. Both of these are on the outside and also on the inside of the front door."

Horwell nodded. "OK, so both persons pushed the door open and also pulled the door shut?"

"But one of them, and obviously it is the first one, left the door open. But why," Detective Menkin said. "Was that done deliberately for the killer to gain access? If so, then it is possible that the first and second person were in cahoots."

Sergeant Horwell nodded: "Interesting thought, and turning to the pathologist he called out, "thanks Doc, and walking to the door motioned Detective Menkin to follow him: "We'll have to have another talk to Henderson and the lady who lives next door. I have a feeling they know more than they have told us."

"What on earth do you think she's done to have two people come after her?" Menkin said. "One belting her up and the other killing her."

"Yes, you wonder. It's interesting though about the size of hands. And I think because of that we can eliminate Henderson from the murder. But he was there, had the argument and roughed her up."

"Yes, and she gave him a split lip," Menkin added.

"Yes," Horwell said. "And it must have been him that left the door open. And I want to know why. But the lady next door is much more interesting. She's got small hands and she knows more than she has told us so far."

"So, we've got a couple of questions here. The first one is: Why was she belted up? I think we know by who, but why? The second question is why was she killed and who did the killing? And this is a bit more difficult. But I think we'll begin by having Mr Henderson and Mrs Freeman fingerprinted."

"Yeah, let's start with them. You know," Menkin said. "The whole thing puzzles me. For Henderson to belt her up.

OK he probably thinks he's got a good reason to do that. But Mrs Freeman. I can't understand why a classy woman like her wants to kill her neighbour. There are other ways if you don't want to live next door to one. The whole thing doesn't add up."

CHAPTER 31

Alice had a dilemma and it was on her mind during the day and it robbed her of her sleep at night. Should she tell the police what she had seen when she was in the stairwell. But then she might have to explain why she had been there at that time of night. But what could they do? There was no law against sitting in the stairwell. But it worried Alice. 'You're not going to sit in a dark stairwell hoping something was going to happen unless you had a fair idea that indeed something was going to happen.'

Another thing that worried Alice was that if she didn't tell the police what she knew and they somehow found out her involvement, could they charge her with withholding evidence and could she go to jail for that? And she was certainly not prepared to go to jail for Ingrid. If she could only talk to somebody, Alice thought, sitting in her kitchen, staring at a cupboard sipping coffee.

Yes, this was another thing this woman had made her do, bullied into, Alice preferred to think, drinking coffee. Now she even liked it and nothing had happened to her. Alice sighed deeply. What was she to do? She should go to the police.

But Ingrid was her friend!

Alice considered that for a moment. Was she really a friend? A companion. Yes, somebody to go to the movies with, or a luncheon. But a friend!? Alice let that thought hang for a moment. What is she really to me? Do I owe her? The word 'loyalty' interrupted and Alice thought about that for a few moments, but then dismissed it with a shrug: 'I don't owe her anything,' she said, half aloud to herself. 'Not a thing.' She had to say it several times to convince herself. Was it because she was scared of Ingrid?

Certainly Ingrid made her feel inferior. She had felt like this for some time now and she wondered if it was because of Ingrid's status, the rich woman from Mosman.

Apart from the misgivings Alice had, she had also been flattered to have been chosen by this woman to go to the movies with her and the odd luncheon, until it began to dawn on Alice that apparently she was good enough for those outings, but just not quite good enough to join her and her society mates to go to the opera and ballet. Not that she had wanted to go but it would have been nice to have been asked. Oh yes, Ingrid had suggested she'd go to these things but not with her. Alice realized and was very conscious of the fact that her manners lacked refinement, but, she thought, 'I'm not putting on airs and graces I don't have.'

Alice sighed, this doesn't get me any closer to my problem. Should I or should I not go to the police. The answer to that was really that she should. She had seen Ingrid go in but of course that didn't mean she had killed the woman. But if she had found the woman dead she should have come out straight away and call the police. But she had stayed inside for quite some time and when she came out she had looked furtively about her, as if she had something to hide, closed the door and had quickly gone into her apartment.

Alice nodded, 'Yes, I have to tell the police what I know. I am morally obliged to do that.' But deep, deep down Alice knew that telling the police had little to do with moral obligations. Alice wanted to get back at Ingrid, make her suffer for the humiliations Ingrid had, in Alice's mind, inflicted upon her. Alice took a deep breath. She had made her decision.

CHAPTER 32

It was not an easy decision but it was the only one. 'Go and see Emma and tell her what he should have told her even before Saskia had begun to visit her. He didn't want to hide behind lies and falsehoods anymore and keep on denying that he knew the woman.

Emma had given the impression that she believed him but he knew she had her doubts. Anyway it probably would all come out now and it was better that he got in first. The deciding factor to see Emma and tell all, had been the photo of the murdered Saskia in the newspaper. God knows what Emma could have been thinking.

Alan turned left into Reserve Road and drove down to the car park having to go up several floors before he found an empty space to put his car. After turning off the engine he remained seated, thinking about Saskia, his affair with her and how to explain his behaviour to Emma. Was he sorry? Yes, very sorry about having cheated on Emma and lying to her.

But was he sorry about Saskia and his affair with her? Alan thought about that for a few moments and he was surprised to find that he wasn't. In fact, if he was really honest with himself, he had to admit it had been rather enjoyable. This relationship with another woman, everything so totally different from Emma, especially the sex. But he was also angry, angry and worried. Angry that she would not take 'no' for an answer when he wanted to finish it because she wanted more and there was no future in that.

He was not going to give up Emma, not for her, not for anybody else. He loved her too much. And he was worried, deeply worried about how all this had turned out with this woman getting murdered and his involvement with her. Alan took a deep breath. 'Well, I'd better be going and face Emma.'

As he went past the nurse's desk he heard his name being called but being preoccupied on seeing Emma he ignored it.

Stepping inside Emma's room he called out: "Hallo darling, how –" the rest of the greeting stuck in his throat when he saw the made-up empty bed and the room tidy. The flowers were still there as were her get-well cards and 4 paperbacks now neatly stacked at the back of the bedside table. It didn't look like Emma was going to come back any moment.

Stunned Alan looked at it for some moments before it actually sunk in: "No," he cried out in despair, "she's --, oh God no, she's gone, she's gone," he cried out. "What has happened, what have they done with her?" Deeply worried Alan hurried back to the front desk and glaring at a nurse sitting behind a computer he demanded angrily: "What's going on, where is my wife?"

"I tried to get your attention as you walked past, but you wouldn't listen," the nurse said. "We also phoned your home but you had obviously left and your mobile was not on. Dr Carlson wants to see you. I've told doctor you're here and he will come to see you shortly."

Unable to sit down, his mind agitated by various emotions, Alan kept pacing back and forth in front of the desk and after several minutes as he was about to approach the nurse again to ask her 'what the hell was keeping the doctor,' he saw him coming down the corridor and went to meet him.

"Sorry, so –" Dr Carlson began. But Alan, furious at not knowing what was going on and even more furious at having been kept waiting, cut him short, and raising his voice angrily, said: "What the hell is going on, doctor? Where is my wife? I want to speak to her now."

"Please come with me, Mr Henderson," Dr Carlson said, calmly, ignoring his outburst and led Alan into a small room with a desk and a few chairs. Pointing to a chair in front of the desk, Dr Carlson said: "Please sit down, Mr Henderson."

Glaring at the doctor, it looked as if Alan was going to ignore the invitation, but then he sat down.

Looking directly at Alan, Dr Carlson said: "There has been a development in your wife's condition and at the moment she is in intensive care."

Alan held Dr Carlson's gaze but after a few moments of intense silence he lowered his eyes.

"So what's wrong with my wife now?" Alan said aggressively, furious at having lost the battle of wills. "She was ready to come home. So what the hell have you people been doing to her?"

Dr Carlson didn't answer. Instead he kept his gaze firmly on Alan, and Alan after a few long moments realized the doctor was not going to be intimidated and that he wouldn't get very far by being aggressive.

Alan forced himself to calm down and taking a deep breath said: "OK sorry. I'm upset. I'm angry as you probably can understand. So, I'll ask again. What has happened?

"Why is she suddenly in intensive care? Are you going to tell me?"

Dr Carlson nodded: "Yes, OK. In the Sunday newspaper there was a photo of a murdered woman."

Alan leant forward and opened his mouth to comment on that but the doctor held up his hand: "Please hear me out, Mr Henderson. Now, the duty nurse at the time informed me that that morning Mrs Henderson was in good spirits, feeling well and looking forward to her breakfast. When a little later the nurse went back into Mrs Henderson's room she found her lying on her back, white as a sheet, her breakfast untouched and a hand lying on the photo of the murdered woman.

"Indeed Mr Henderson, your wife was ready to go home. She wasn't sick. What happened to her had nothing to do with why she was in hospital. Something or somebody upset her so much that she collapsed. We have reason to believe that it was because of the photo in the newspaper. I have been told that this lady used to visit your wife. And I must tell you that the death of a relative, however close the relationship, would not cause that what has happened to your wife. Now Mr Henderson, I hope you can shed some light on this because unless we know what has happened, we will not know how to treat it."

Occasionally shifting uneasily in his chair, Alan Henderson had been listening to Dr Carlson in growing disquiet. His arrogant, demanding behaviours which had marked the beginning of the talk had turned into meek acceptance of the doctor's authority.

While the doctor was talking a picture of what must have happened had formed in Alan's mind. Emma had looked at the photo of the murdered woman, recognised Saskia and immediately assumed that her husband had killed her. Alan was sure, in spite of his denials Emma had been suspecting for some time now, that there was a connection and that something had been going on between them. And if he had been honest about it and had told her the truth; Emma could now be coming home instead of being in intensive care.

The thought that through his stupid behaviour he may now well lose Emma was too much to bear. Guilt and remorse hit him hard and unable to control his emotion, Alan put his hands against his face and cried.

Sparing Alan the embarrassment of being watched Dr Carlson got up and left the room. When he returned some

10 minutes later; he put a glass of water in front of Alan: "Drink some," he said. "It'll do you good."

Nodding gratefully Alan drank the water and putting the glass back on the desk, he cleared his throat and looking at the doctor he said: "This is going to be very difficult."

There was a long silence when Alan finished talking. He had not spared himself. At last the doctor spoke: "Thank you for telling me. Now I understand her sudden collapse and maybe we can do something about it."

"Can I see her?"

Dr Carlson nodded. "Sure, come with me. I must warn you though, you may get a shock!"

It shocked Alan to the core to see Emma lying there still, her face a white mask. He looked at Dr Carlson who motioned Alan to follow him out of the room.

"Now I know what happened," he said. "I am reasonably certain she will come out of it. What had happened was that, on seeing the photo of the dead woman Emma knew as Sassie and who she had suspected of being involved with her husband that, in order to stop Saskia talking to her, you had killed her. The inability to cope with the reality of this shut down her brain. Medically there is really nothing we can do. It's up to you now. Talk to her and keep talking. Keep telling her all is well, the house, the garden, the weather, you yourself, the neighbours and every once in a while, tell her that you did not kill Sassie. You had nothing to do with it. She can hear you. Stay with her, hold her hand and keep talking. If you need help let me know. OK? Bye for now."

"Yes, thanks doctor."

Alan went a bit closer to the bed and now noticed Emma was breathing. After another lingering look Alan went back into the corridor and phoned his secretary. He told her he would not be coming in for the rest of the week.

He also got onto his solicitor and explained what had happened.

It was now the third day after Alan had told Dr Carlson his story and the rest of that day and up to now Alan had, at Dr Carlson's suggestion, been back at the hospital morning and afternoon sitting next to Emma's bed, holding her hand and talking to her about everything the doctor had suggested.

But there were times he would just sit there, next to her holding her hand and looking at her with tears welling up in his eyes. With the guilt of what he had done to her and the hurt he had caused her overwhelmed him.

And now, late in the afternoon on the third day Alan thought he saw a movement in her eyelids. He had been babbling on about the house, the neighbours and the garden and again that he had not killed Sassie, when he thought he saw it. Alan stopped talking as if not to disturb that moment, staring hard at her eyes.

"Can you hear me?" he said at last. "Can you hear what I am saying, I did not kill Sassie, please believe me." Then he felt it, or at least he thought he felt it; a slight, an ever, ever so slight tightening of her fingers. A jolt surged through him. Could it be? Did she really hear and believed what I said?

Then he saw it again, the slight twitch in her eyelids and again he felt the squeeze, the ever so slight squeeze on his hand. It was there, he was absolutely sure now. She was here! She was back! Then he felt it again and this time it was a definite tightening of her fingers around his hand then, after taking a deep breath Emma opened her eyes and looked at Alan. Slowly Alan became aware he was sitting in a chair with his hands in his lap, and touching a glass and his head felt as if a bomb had gone off in it. He opened his eyes but the light in the room made it feel as if a second bomb had gone off. He lifted a hand to his head, pressing

135

and rubbing it to try to ease the pain. Again he opened his eyes, but a fraction now and squinted about the room. 'OK, so he was home, but, and this was scary, he had no idea how he got there.'

He just sat for a few moments thinking, trying to recall how he got into the situation he was in now. His body seemed to be locked in the shape of the chair and shifting about made him winch. Yes, he had gone to the hospital to see Emma. That's right, he remembered now. He was with Emma when she opened her eyes. So he must have been at the hospital and he must have driven from the hospital to his home, except that he could not remember anything about that.

Slowly, bit by bit Alan began to recall what happened. Yes, that's right. Emma had opened her eyes. He had been so excited about that and he also remembered shouting for joy but then Emma had taken her hand out of his and closed her eyes again. Frowning he remember staring at her, dumbfounded, not believing she would do that.

He had grabbed her hand again and almost shouting said: "No, no, please Emma, please don't do this, and yes," sobbing he had kept on, "please Emma don't. I love you. I love you so very much. I am sorry, so very sorry. It wasn't me. You must believe me."

But Emma had kept her eyes closed and had slipped her hands under the cover, out of his reach. It was then that he remembered her look. What he had expected had been a look of love and understanding. Instead it had been accusing. It had said what had been gnawing away at his conscience "What have you done to me?" Then and only then he had fully realized what she must have been going through. What he really had seen in her eyes when she opened them was not only hurt, pain and anguish but also anger, anger at the man who had betrayed her love. Not knowing what to do he had kept staring at Emma.

Tears in his eyes, mumbling: "Please look at me, please please." But Emma had not responded and in the end he had rung the bell. When not only the nurse but also the doctor arrived Alan deeply distraught and teary told them: "She opened her eyes; she looked at me and then she took her hand out of mine and closed her eyes again."

"My God." Alan shook his head and winced as the muscles in his neck protested at the movement. 'How bloody embarrassing, standing there like a little whimpering school boy telling tales.'

Alan scoffed at the doctor's nodded understanding, as he took Alan gently by the arm leading him away from the bed saying: "Now Mr Henderson, would you mind leaving us for a while. Go and get yourself a cup of coffee and maybe something to eat. It looks like you can do with some. We'll come and get you when we are ready."

'Yes' he remembered alright. He had nodded in agreement and meekly gone to the coffee shop. But he had been angry, upset and embarrassed, especially embarrassed at his behaviour. No wonder the doctor had talked to him as he did. What he bloody well should have told the doctor, he thought, getting angry again: 'I'm bloody well seeing my wife when I want to see her and not when you tell me to. She is my wife.'

But he hadn't and he remembered sitting in the coffee shop staring darkly into his coffee cup, fuming, till the nurse came and told him that Emma was now out of danger and had been moved back to her old room.

"Can I see her," he had asked. "Sure, but no talking or touching."

Alan nodded that he understood and stayed just inside the door. He remembered looking at Emma lying there, very still and very pale. He just stood there and

137

looked, feeling guilty and full of remorse, till the nurse touched him, telling him that time was up.

The doctor had been waiting for Alan at the desk and leading him away from there told Alan that they would keep Emma till at least the end of the week and that they would reassess to see if she was ready to go home.

"Can I come and see her?"

A renewed flash of anger welled up in him as he remembered how he had asked that. Meekly, apologetically almost: 'What's happening to me?,' he asked himself, anger still burning in him, 'that I let myself be intimidated and treated like some, some ignorant nobody?'

"Sure," the doctor had answered in his authoritive, patronizing voice: "But, er – leave it for a couple of days. Wait till Wednesday and then give us a call and the nurse will tell you if it is OK to come. Look Mr Henderson," the doctor said to Alan in an annoyingly, patronizing voice. Adding insult to injury: "Let's be frank. From what you have told me your wife has been through a lot and this needs time to heal, mentally as well as physically. You will have to be patient."

Alan remembered nodding, looking past the doctor at something, he couldn't remember what, on the wall behind him and that he had said: "Well, I had better go now, feeling a raging anger building up inside him, an anger that felt like smashing everything and everybody, especially the doctor in sight.

And now he was back home and no idea how he got there. The last thing he remembered was walking away from the doctor; before he was going to smash his face in. Anything in between that and now sitting in the chair was a blank.

Alan sighed, a deep resigning sigh. Sitting here thinking about it doesn't get me anywhere. Grimacing, Alan gingerly pushed himself out of his chair and slowly stretched his back out of its locked position. 'Bloody hell,' he muttered, 'I must have been in that chair for a good 12 or 13 hours. No wonder every muscle and bone in my body is protesting.' His eyes fell on the almost empty Scotch bottle on the table. 'My God,' he called out, 'I must have drunk half the bloody bottle.'

About an hour later, after a hot shower, a couple of cups of coffee and something to eat, Alan felt much better. And after taking a couple of Panadol the pain in his head was slowly disappearing.

After cleaning up Alan phoned his secretary: "Liza, look. Yes, I'm alright thank you. How are you? Good, well I won't be coming in for the rest of the week. There has been a set-back with – no, nothing serious but I'd like to be on hand if they need me. If there is anything that needs my attention, could you scan or email it through. Thank you Liza. I'll be in touch during the week. Bye now."

Alan sat for a few moments, phone in hand, suddenly feeling very tired. It was as if every ounce of energy had drained out of his body. He replaced the phone and practically dragged himself upstairs to the bedroom. He got as far as taking off his shoes and trousers and loosened his tie before he slumped down on the bed, immediately falling soundly asleep till well into the afternoon.

The next morning Alan had just finished cleaning up after his breakfast and was ready to go upstairs to his study when the phone rang. Alan looked at his watch, noting it was just after 8 and wondered who would be ringing him at this time in the morning. But, as he took the phone off its station; a jolt of anxiety went through him as the word 'Hospital' flashed through his mind.

"Yes," he said, his voice betraying his angst. "Mr Henderson, Senior Constable Menkin here."

The sigh of relief was clearly audible, prompting Senior Constable Menkin to ask: "Are you alright, Mr Henderson?"

"Yes, yes, I'm alright. I'm fine, thank you."

"Mr Henderson, I wonder if you can come to Sydney City, this morning and provide a DNA sample and to be fingerprinted. And we'd also like to ask you a few questions. I'm sure you'll prefer that than for us to come and pick you up?"

"Yes indeed. Thank you. I'll be there." Alan put the phone down, thinking: 'That's all very well agreeing to do this but I will need Neville there with me. And the bugger is always busy. Anyway, here goes.'

"Neville, Alan here. Er – look. I've been asked to see the police at Sydney City this morning for a DNA and fingerprinting and they also want to ask me a few more questions. Can you come and meet me there?"

After a short silence Neville said: "Give me an hour and I'll be there."

After the DNA swab and fingerprinting Alan and his solicitor were taken to an interview room. After a few minutes Sergeant Horwell and Senior Constable Menkin walked in. Following introductions Sergeant Horwell said: "We just want to clear up a few things. You're not under arrest and you haven't been charged. You don't have to answer any of the questions but it will help us if you do. We found the deceased's diary. Are you the Alan Henderson mentioned in the diary?"

"Yes."

"Were you there on that Friday evening and why?"

"I went to see her to ask her to stop writing letters to me. In fact to ask her not to get in contact with me in any form ever again."

"Why would she want to write letters to you?"

"We had an affair. I broke it off and she wasn't happy about that. And she kept writing letters."

"So you went to her apartment to ask her to stop writing letters to you. What about a phone call?"

"I tried, several times, but when she heard my voice she hung up."

"Did you assault her?"

Alan glanced at Neville, who nodded. "No, I just slapped her."

"Why?"

"Well, she kept saying she was going to tell my wife and that I couldn't stop her from doing that. She said it several times, taunting me and I lost my temper. But I can assure you when I left she was very much alive. She had fallen down and was on the floor but she was alive. I had made sure of that. I left her then. When I got to the front door I could hear voices but there was nobody around. I went to the lift leaving the front door open in case I had to go back inside. I didn't want anybody to know I had been there. I could have gone back and closed the door when the lift arrived but I didn't. I was too anxious to get into that lift and get out of there. And something else. I read in the newspaper that she was found in the bathroom. Well, as I have said before, when I left she was very much alive in the lounge-room. I have nothing more to add."

CHAPTER 33

"There is a lady to see you, Sarge," the young constable said, standing in the doorway of his office.

"What is it about?"

"She wants to talk to the person in charge of the investigation of the murder of Miss Birman."

"OK. I'll talk to her." Sergeant Horwell pushed his chair away from his desk and followed the constable.

"That's her, Sarge," the constable pointed to Alice, who was nervously pulling on a handkerchief and dabbing her face with it.

"Good morning. I'm Sergeant Horwell. What can I do for you, Mrs – er – Mrs – er?"

"Miss," Alice corrected. "Miss Murphy." And looking about her furtively she added: "Um – er – can we – er – can we go somewhere less public please?"

"Sure," Sergeant Horwell said, leading Alice into a small room with a table and three chairs off the main corridor.

Alice was still feeling guilty dobbing in her friend, which, she kept reminded herself, is not really her friend and she has to protect herself. She doesn't want to go to prison for withholding information and she had convinced herself that, if the tables were turned, Ingrid would put her in quick as a flash.

"Can I get you a cup of tea or a cup of coffee?"

Looking everywhere but at the Sergeant, Alice said: "No, no, thank you."

Horwell was well aware of Alice's nervousness and waited patiently for Alice to settle down, recognising that what she was going to tell him must be very difficult for her.

Finally, putting her hands in her lap and leaning back, Alice, taking a deep breath and now looking at the Sergeant said: "I saw her go in."

"Saw who go in?"

"Ingrid, - er – Mrs Freeman."

"Where were you?"

"I – er – I – er – I was sitting on the steps in the stairwell, watching the woman's front door."

Frowning questioningly Sergeant Horwell inclined his head.

"We were watching to see what was going to happen. Now the businessman, that's how we identified him, had gone to see her," Alice explained. "You see, he had been watching from across the road all week. We thought she had given him the boot and he was trying to go back to her."

"Where was Mrs Freeman?"

"Watching from her apartment. I had phoned her that he was on his way. Anyway, the businessman got in and there was some shouting and then he left, dabbing his lips with a tissue or a handkerchief."

"How long do you think he was inside?"

"Oh, I don't know, not very long. Maybe about 10 minutes. Maybe a bit more. It seemed to be all over very quickly. Anyway, for some reason he left the front door open and when the lift came he went.

"OK I thought getting up, I'll go in and have a look to see what has happened in there, when Ingrid came out of her apartment quickly and went into the woman's place and pulled the door shut. Now, you see, if I had been a bit faster I would have got in there with her and probably could have saved the woman."

"Saved? What do you mean? How?"

"Well, from Ingrid. She hated the whore, as she called her. The woman was a call girl you know, an escort and we thought she was giving the apartment a bad name."

"So you think it was Mrs Freeman who killed Miss Birman? How long do you think Mrs Freeman was inside?"

"Oh, I don't know exactly, but it was quite some time."

"15 minutes? 20 minutes?" Sergeant Horwell offered.

"Oh, it was more than 10 minutes. I was getting stiff sitting in that stairwell. You know I wanted to leave but I also wanted to see her coming out."

Sergeant Horwell nodded understandingly.

Alice was now really in a telling mode. She had to get it out. All the pent-up frustrations had to find an outlet and this was it.

"Well," Alice continued. "You know I wondered what she was doing in there all that time. You know, just to have a look to see what had happened in there is one thing but being in there for that length of time – well! Then I thought maybe she is helping the woman. You know, like giving first aid. But then, you know, I was getting stiff and I was getting sore as well. So I thought that's it. I'm leaving and just as I was about to get up, very slowly as you can imagine, she came out. I mean Ingrid, looking sort of, you know, left and right. Then she pulled the door shut and hurried back to her apartment.

"Well, I thought that doesn't look as if she has helped the poor woman, more like she's killed her. You know, I've done some thinking."

"Yes, go on, Sergeant Horwell gave an encouraging nod.

"Well, I thought, if the woman had been dead she wouldn't have had to spend so much time in there. If she had been badly injured she would have got the ambulance. And if everything had been alright; the woman would have let her out and closed the door. So, when I heard later that the woman had been killed I knew she'd done it."

Alice stopped. Little beads of perspiration began to form on her face and plucking nervously at her handkerchief she looked at Sergeant Horwell. She felt very guilty now having let her mouth get ahead of her brain, babbling on. She shouldn't have said all this. She didn't know what Ingrid had been doing. What was going to happen now?

Would they lock her up because she had waited so long before she had told them?

Sergeant Horwell cut into her thoughts. "Thank you very much Miss Murphy for telling me this. We will look into it. Now, would you be prepared to tell this to a judge in court?" Sergeant Horwell asked, switching off the recorder.

Mortified Alice looked at Sergeant Horwell and then at the recorder. She hadn't noticed it. "Oh dear, oh dear. Oh, I don't know. I don't like her to know I told you all this."

"But you had to tell us Miss Murphy. This is a murder investigation and we have to know everything about it, every detail. You have been very helpful. Thank you for coming in. Mrs Freeman will understand. If it was the other way around she would have done the same thing, it is your duty. Now, don't you worry. Everything will be alright. Are you alright for transport? Can I get one of the officers to drop you off home?"

Alarmed Alice looked at Sergeant Horwell. 'Being taken home by the police! What would Ingrid think if she saw it? "Oh no, thank you sir. Thank you very much. It is not far and I have to do some shopping."

CHAPTER 34

Emma had said her thank you's and goodbye's and now, resting her arm on Alan's they walked out of the private hospital to the car park. That Emma put her hand on his arm to lead her out of the hospital surprised Alan, as he thought back on the harrowing two days before this.

"Emma can go home tomorrow," Dr Carlson had told Alan when he was about to leave late Thursday afternoon. "She is well but fragile," he had added, leaving no doubt as to what he meant.

Alan had merely nodded and walked away still very tempted to smash his face in.

Wednesday had been the first day the doctor had allowed Alan to come and visit Emma. As he entered the room Alan saw her sitting in a chair near the window. He had almost walked up to her to kiss her but he didn't, afraid she might turn her head. So Alan sat down on the chair on the other side of the bed.

There had been no acknowledgement from Emma that he had arrived and after a few moments shifting uncomfortably in his chair, Alan finally said: "How are you?" When there was no response, he added: "You are looking well."

Emma now turned her head and looked at Alan. A dark, angry withering look and turned back to look through the window again.

Alan nodded, sadly. 'What did he expect? An open arm welcome?' Sighing he realized she wasn't going to make it easy for him. He had known that, even before he had gone to the hospital. Alan had never seen her like that. They'd had their arguments, disagreements and there had been times Emma had been very very angry. But nothing like this. This was a side of Emma he hadn't known existed.

She probably hadn't even known about this side of her herself.

Alan felt it coming, slowly building up inside him. This anger, this all-consuming anger, a rage, stored up inside him every day and now fuelled by Emma ignoring him, nearly made him pick up the chair he was sitting on and smash it against the wall. But with almost super-human restraint he held himself in check. 'Don't lose your cool,' he counselled himself. 'Remember who the real victim is here. Don't get angry at her stubbornness and thus make it more difficult to reconcile.' For Alan was sure she would. She had not refused to see him. But she was going to make him suffer.

Alan stared at Emma and in spite of his anger, his body was hurting with love for her. But she was just sitting there, cold as ice, looking out the window. The silence, the tension began to get to Alan. He thought he was really going to blow up if she didn't say something, anything.

Finally, in desperation, he cried out: "Emma, please!" After a long moment Emma turned her head and looked at Alan.

"Yes Alan!" The voice was cold, polite.

But the relief to hear her voice was immense. Alan's taut, strained body sagged and a deep sigh escaped his lungs. At last she had spoken.

But Emma wasn't going to give in, not just yet. She would, she knew she would in the end. Her love for him was strong. Too strong for his betrayal of her trust to let destroy the bond they had between them. She had seen his state of distress but she felt not sorry, no remorse for doing this to him. Emma believed him when he said he had not killed Saskia but what he had done to her was beyond belief. Never in her life had she thought it possible he would do this to her. Yes, she remembered talking about it to Marjorie many months ago, but not really believing that

Alan would do this. But he had. However, she believed him when he had said he would never do this to her again.

———————————————

Alan unlocked the car and opened the passenger front door. Emma accepting the gesture said, "Thank you" and sat down.

The trip home was made in silence although several times during the drive Alan had been on the verge of telling Emma how wonderful it was to have her back home again, but glancing at Emma occasionally, told him that that was not a good idea. Even though the expression on her face gave no indication of her inner feelings, there was something in her whole demeanour that stopped him.

It was only after he had parked the car and they had gone inside and were standing in the lounge-room that Emma spoke and what she said took Alan completely by surprise. "I would appreciate it if you would sleep in the guest bedroom. You can start taking your belongings out of the bedroom now. Let me know when you are finished." All the while her gaze had been steady on Alan who, after a moment's hesitation, without a word, strode past Emma and went upstairs.

As he was going up it also occurred to him that she had not said: "For the time being or, our bedroom." Thinking about that made him angry and by the time he got to the top of the stairs he was ropeable. 'Who the bloody hell did she think she was ordering – him, her husband, out of their bedroom, out of our bedroom?' For a few long moments he stood on the landing, fuming. 'Ignore it. Go back down and tell her I'm not doing it.' Alan pondered about that for a few moments. 'Be careful about that' he cautioned himself. The way Emma had told him to move out allowed no argument, unless he wanted a ding-dong row on his hands.

And just now that was the last thing he wanted. It also suddenly occurred to him that the way she was obviously feeling now, she could say: 'OK, I'll move out.' And she would. Alan knew her well enough for that. And then there was no telling when he'd get her back. Calming down Alan thought about that for a few moments and finally, much as it dented his ego, he decided to accept the inevitable. Alan nodded resignedly. 'Yes, it was better if he moved out.'

CHAPTER 35

Putting the finishing touches of make-up on her face and putting a few imaginary wayward locks of her still golden brown hair into place; Ingrid picked up her handbag to go down to the car park when the doorbell rang. She stopped, wondering as to who it could be at this time of the morning. She looked at her watch, not quite 7.45am, just past 7.30am. She didn't move. Maybe they'd go away. After a few moments the doorbell rang again. This time longer, sounding urgent. Whoever it was hadn't gone away and she really couldn't ignore it any longer. She had to get out through the front door to get to the car park. She was on her way to a game of golf at Monash. She had only played there a couple of times on invitation and she was looking forward to playing there again very much. And it was not only a game of golf she was looking forward too, out of the blue one of the now retired directors from her husband's firm had phoned her inviting her to a game of golf at Monash. His wife had died some 3 years ago and slowly he had gone back to normal living, as much as that was possible without her companionship.

Why Ingrid was so keen was, she had, apart from a game of golf, also something else in mind. The businessman had stirred up a feeling inside her and ever since, this had been constantly on her mind, and, what was more annoying, wanting it. His phone call had been a god send. She was sure he wasn't passed it. OK then! Ready to put off anybody who wanted to engage her in whatever, Ingrid opened the door, to two well-dressed men she instantly recognised as the detectives she had spoken to before. With the curt: "Yes?" Ingrid's face clearly displayed her intense displeasure at being disturbed at this time in the morning without previously being notified.

"Good morning, madam, Sergeant Horwell said. "I'm sure you do remember us, Mrs Freeman? I wonder if we may have a word please, inside?"

"I don't see the need for that," Ingrid said, getting angry, "I have nothing to add to what I have already told you and I would rather you go away now. I have an urgent appointment this morning and I don't want to be late for it."

Sergeant Horwell exchanged a glance with Senior Constable Menkin who nodded and said: "Well, I'm sorry about that Mrs Freeman, but there are several matters regarding the murder of Ms Birman we'd like to clear up and for us to do that we would like you to come with us. I suggest you phone your solicitor and see if he can come to assist you when we interview you. And I also suggest that you cancel your appointment. We would like to take your fingerprints and get a DNA sample."

"I will do no such thing," Ingrid answered, raising her voice, now really getting angry. "What I want you to do is to go away. I have better things to do than talk to police about something I have already said about all I know." But Ingrid had noted the change in tone and manner. From asking they were now telling her and they were not going to take 'no' for an answer. For several long moments, eyes flashing, jaw set, Ingrid stared at them, then, taking a deep breath, she nodded resignedly. And although outwardly calm and unfazed her heart had skipped a beat, had they found something? It couldn't be, she had been so careful, then she remembered pushing open and closing the front door. They didn't have her fingerprints and that's what they wanted now. She would now have to tell them that she had been inside.

Sergeant Horwell raised his eyebrows enquiringly.

"Er, yes, er – OK. I'm sorry. It's all just a bit unexpected. Please come in. I'll make my phone call now."

Trying to not show her nervousness, Ingrid went into the study to make her phone call.

After arriving at the police station Ingrid was taken to an interview room to wait for her solicitor, Mr Harold Green, who upon arrival was taken straight to Ingrid.

Some 20 minutes later the detectives entered the room and after introducing themselves to the solicitor, they switched on the recorder.

Following formal introduction of time and who was present, Sergeant Horwell began his questions.

"On that Friday night you heard arguing and screaming?"

"Yes."

"What did you do? Did you phone the police? Did you have a look to see what was going on?"

"I didn't think it was any of my business."

"I suggest to you that you did have a look. You noticed the front door open and you went inside. ."

Ingrid looked at her solicitor. She had already told him what she was now going to tell the detectives.

"Well, first of all I didn't want to get involved but OK yes, this is what happened. I went to my front door to see what was going on and was just in time to see a man coming out of the apartment."

"Did you recognize the man?"

"Yes. It was the same man who had been standing on the street watching the building. I believe at one stage they had a relationship."

"And what did you do next?"

"Well, I noticed he had left the front door open and I wondered if I should go in to see if she needed help. So I did go inside and found the woman dead in the bathroom. There was nothing I could do for her and I left. I was pretty upset but I didn't report it because I didn't want to get involved and it could have been construed that I had killed the woman. And when I left the apartment yes, I shut the front door. I did that without thinking about it."

Sergeant Horwell nodded: "Yeah. Er, show me your hands please?" Ingrid held out her hands.

"Thank you. You play golf, tennis, you go to the gym? Would you say you are a very fit and strong woman?"

Ingrid looked at her solicitor. "What does this have to do with the murder of the woman?" Mr Green asked.

"How long do you think you were inside the apartment, Mrs Freeman?" Detective Menkin asked, ignoring the solicitor.

"Oh, I don't know, maybe one, two minutes at the most three, the lights were on."

"Did you know exactly where to find her?" Detective Constable Menkin said.

"Well, yes, er – no, er – well I couldn't see her, so I guessed she'd be in the bathroom."

"Yes," Detective Sergeant Horwell said. "That was a good guess. Miss Birman was in the bathroom obviously cleaning her face and hands and about to put balm on when you surprised her. I suggest to you that you found her very much alive. You were not in her apartment for one or two minutes. You were in there for a good 15 to 20 minutes. Enough time to put your hands around Miss Birman's throat and strangle her. Mrs Freeman, I'm arresting you for the murder of Saskia Birman. You do not ...."

"This is outrageous, preposterous," Mr Green shouted, getting to his feet. "How dare you suggest this monstrous accusation to my client?"

Ingrid sat motionless, blankly, staring ahead. She gave no indication that she had heard what Sergeant Horwell had said.

It was as if the words had come from a great distance. They had taken a long time to come, over 40 years, and they had been spoken to that other person that was harbouring within her, that other person she had not really been able to get rid of.

They had not been spoken to Ingrid Freeman but to Ingrid Larsdon, the killer of a prostitute in Norway. This person had been strangled and it was always assumed it had been done by a client, which, in a way, was right. The young woman prostitute had destroyed her father who had frequented them after his wife, her mother, had died. Then he had taken a shine to one of them and she had taken him for everything he had. Ingrid, who was 22 years at the time knew about it and watched her father being destroyed. Mentally, physically and financially and finally killing himself.

Ingrid phoned him every day around 10 o'clock to check on him and sometimes, work permitting, take him to lunch. This one day he didn't answer his phone and Ingrid, worried, had gone to his apartment. She had a key, but she always rang the bell first, a special ring to let him know it was her. When, after some time, he hadn't come to the door Ingrid let herself in, calling out to find where he was. She found him in the bathroom, in the bath, the water red with his blood. He had slashed his wrists.

Ingrid didn't remember what happened after finding her father like that, but when she finally regained consciousness she found herself on the floor next to the bath, her hands red with his blood.

Even after all these years, reliving this terrible moment in her life still made Ingrid shudder with emotion. Trying to hold back the tears that welled up in her eyes she again felt deeply the guilt for not looking after him, helping him, as she should have. She should have moved in with him. It was when she got up off the floor and with a last look at her father, that she made the vow to find that prostitute and kill her.

After the funeral Ingrid went through his belongings and when going through his papers; had a good idea where to find her and after a couple of weeks searching and asking, she had found her. The rest had been easy.

One night Ingrid had walked up to her and asked if she did girl stuff. She did and when they got to the prostitute's apartment, Ingrid strangled her. She had already made provisions to leave and within five days she was on her way to Australia.

In Australia she met Mr Freeman, got married and over a period of time to put that episode of her life so far back in her memory she had all but forgotten about it. But Saskia and the businessman had brought it all back. The well-dressed businessman, her father, the prostitute; Saskia, and with it again came the hate, the all-consuming hate for a person in that profession.

Ingrid suddenly blinked and shook her head as if to shake something away and looked at Detective Sergeant Horwell.

"We know you hated her," Detective Sergeant Horwell said, "and we have a witness who will testify about the time you spent inside and it wasn't just a couple of minutes, more like 20 minutes, maybe even more."

Ingrid raised her eyebrows questioningly, then she nodded.

'Of course, Alice. That woman must have been talking to them. Alice must have watched her going in and waited for her to come out. Miss Goody, Goody Church Goer. Why oh why did she even associate with that plebian nobody? Ingrid shook her head, despairingly. And only because she wanted someone to go to the movies with. She should have kept within her own milieu.

Ingrid looked at Mr Green who in turn looked at Detective Sergeant Horwell: "Can I have a word with my client please?"

Detective Sergeant Horwell, getting up from his chair, nodded, indicating with his head to Detective Senior Constable Menkin to follow him out.

"Well," Detective Senior Constable Menkin said after closing the door behind them. "This looks pretty cut and dry," to no-one in particular.

There was a hush when Ingrid Freeman was brought into the courtroom. Her eyes downcast she took her seat. The case had had a lot of exposure through the newspapers and on television. A woman in her position and standing in the community accused of murder. Not that Ingrid had seen it, but some of her friends had come to tell her, not believing that this lady whom most of them had known for many years was capable of doing what had been alleged about her.

Not that Ingrid gave anything away and in the end refused to have visitors. Most friends however had already stayed away not wanting to be seen associating with a murderer. One person however Ingrid would have liked to have a word with was Alice. But Alice stayed away. Alice, too scared and embarrassed to face Ingrid also refused to go to the courtroom until it was time for her to give evidence.

Having had sleepless nights before she had told the police about what she knew, now she had had sleepless nights because she felt guilty of having told the police. She had cried because she felt she had betrayed Ingrid. They had been friends. They'd had lovely times together and more often than not Ingrid had picked up the bill for lunches and morning teas.

Ingrid was a skite. OK, so what? If she had done all those things, Alice thought, she'd probably be skiting about it too. But then again, had Ingrid really been skiting or had she merely been talking about places and events she had been to and she Alice had never seen or experienced?

But it was only now because she felt guilty that Alice wanted to see it like that. And a new dribble of tears ran down her cheeks. And now she was here, at court, having to give evidence against a woman who had been her only friend in her adult life and on her evidence most likely sending that woman, her friend, to prison.

But tears were drying up again when, sitting on that bench and thinking about it all; Alice wondered whether she was really sorry and felt pity for Ingrid or did she regret having put herself in this position?

Alice shrugged, wiping the last of her tears off her cheeks. She knew the answer but wouldn't immediately acknowledge it. She wanted to be sorry and feel pity for Ingrid but no matter how she tried she couldn't. Alice wanted Ingrid to suffer because she was still angry and jealous about the life Ingrid had led. Travelling around the world doing and seeing things Alice had never been able to do.

Alice was called to the witness stand and was sworn in. The lawyer in charge of the prosecution stood up and after arranging some papers on the desk in front of him began: "You went to the police to tell them what you saw on the night Miss Birman was killed? And what you saw was the accused going into Miss Birman's apartment and coming out after at least 20 minutes or maybe even longer. Is that true?"

"Yes, timid, with a nod of her head.

"In the days and weeks before that, Mrs Freeman expressed to you her feelings for Miss Birman and that was a feeling of hate and loathing for the 'dirty whore' er – her words Your Honour," the prosecutor said turning to the judge, "and what she would like to do to her when she had her by herself, and that was to strangle her. Is that not true?"

Teary, Alice looked helplessly to the Judge, not really wanting to answer that question because in that they were both guilty.

"Please answer the question, Miss Murphy" "Yes," barely audible.

"Speak up please," sternly from the Judge. "Yes," firm now but teary.

"Well, Miss Murphy, that night Mrs Freeman did have Miss Birman by herself. Don't you think in the circumstances she might have done what she said to you she would do?"

The defense jumped up protesting and the Judge did not allow the question.

"Now Miss Murphy, you told us Mrs Freeman had been inside at least 15 minutes. Weren't you wondering what she was doing in there all that time?"

Looking as if she would burst into tears any moment, Alice nodded. "Speak up please."

"Yes."

"Now, I put it to you, what Mrs Freeman was doing in there was hardly first aid, would you think? Mrs Freeman didn't come out and raise the alarm? No, she shut the door when she went into the apartment, so she couldn't be disturbed as to what she was going to do. That is to kill the occupant in that apartment. Then when she came out of the apartment, looking around furtively, pulling the door shut behind her and hurried back into her apartment. Not the actions of a person who is concerned about the welfare of another person? And the reason for that action was because it was Mrs Freeman who had strangled that woman. No more further questions, Your Honour."

"Miss Murphy, I believe you were good friends with Mrs Freeman?" the lawyer acting for Ingrid began his defence.

Alice nodded. "Speak up please."

"Yes, in a teary voice.

"Mrs Freeman, offering friendship and companionship to a lonely woman was a very kind gesture, was it not?"

"Yes."

"And when you were together, be it for a cup of coffee or a lunch Mrs Freeman occasionally talked about some of the things she had seen or done while overseas, thinking you might be interested, because you have never been anywhere or done anything like that. Is that not so?"

"I don't know," timid voice with a shrug.

"You don't know?" The lawyer's voice was faintly sarcastic.

"Were you envious, or did you feel intimidated, annoyed, angry even at this woman talking like that because in your mind, she was showing off, seeing you never had the chance to go anywhere or do anything like that?"

"No," emphasized, with a shake of the head.

"No!!" The barrister's tone was bordering on sarcasm. "And now you have betrayed that friendship by going to the police telling them that you thought, thought mind you, that Mrs Freeman had killed Miss Birman. Although you had no real proof of that. Oh yes, you know she didn't like Miss Birman because of her profession. But neither did you. And would you have killed Miss Birman?"

"Objection Your Honour, that is a leading question."

"Withdraw Your Honour. Miss Murphy, I suggest to you that you went to the police out of spite, like: Who did this woman think she was by trying to lord it over me with her stories? So you decided to teach this woman a lesson.

159

Oh yes, you saw her going in the apartment and you saw her coming out. Now, you told my learned friend that the period Mrs Freeman had been inside had to be at least 20 minutes, maybe even longer. Did you have a watch on you?"

"No," teary.

"And you were sitting in a dark stairwell on concrete steps feeling very uncomfortable. So, in the dark and in that uncomfortable position seconds can feel like minutes and minutes can feel like hours. So, I suggest to you; you had no idea whatsoever about how long Mrs Freeman had been inside Miss Birman's apartment. That was purely guesswork, was it not?"

Helplessly, tears dribbling down her cheeks, Alice turned towards the judge. "Please answer the question Miss Murphy."

With bowed head and tears still dribbling Alice answered: "Yes."

"No more questions, Your Honour."

"You may step down, Miss Murphy."

On the way back to her seat Alice looked at Ingrid, tears in her eyes and blurted out: "I'm so sorry Ingrid, so very sorry. Please forgive me."

Ingrid looked at Alice, a cold withering look showing no recognition. For Ingrid Alice no longer existed.

CHAPTER 36

Emma opened her eyes and stretched languidly enjoying the luxury of lying in her own bed. Wondering what the time was she lifted her head to look at the bedside clock and was surprised to see it was just after 6.30 a.m. The temptation to just lie back, close her eyes and if she didn't go back to sleep, listen to the 7 o'clock news on the ABC. This appealed to her but maybe she should get up and have breakfast with Alan. Emma thought about that for a moment and then asked herself. Why? This breakfast wouldn't be any different to the lunches and dinners they had over the weekend and why put herself through that? For most of the weekend Alan had been avoiding her, going into his study and closing the door.

Thinking back on it Emma shrugged. OK, so he is not happy. And she was almost certain it was because she had banished him to the guest bedroom. She had wondered sometimes why she had done that. But she had. Done it almost on impulse and she made no excuse for it. Was she punishing him? She thought about that for a moment, then she nodded. Yes! Because just now she could not after all that she knew about Alan's infidelities; carry on as if nothing had happened. And for now at least it had to be the way she wanted it whether Alan liked it or not. She was in control. For how long?

Emma nodded pensively. Yes, when was she going to relent and let him back in her bed again? Because she would, she knew she would. Would it be a week, ten days, fourteen days, longer? Thinking about that, Emma, for a moment, wavered. What was she doing? Was she being stupid, unreasonable? But after a few minutes thinking about that Emma shook her head resolutely. No, she was not; neither stupid or unreasonable. The wound was still very raw and she was still coming to terms with it. And of course it would also depend on Alan and up to now his behaviour had not been such that would make forgiving him easy.

For a fleeting moment she wondered about herself, on her need for him but she dismissed the thought. She wasn't going to give in. She had to be strong. At least for now. Yes, at least for now. Emma remembered what Marjorie had said when she told her what she had done.

Marjorie, after having given it some thought, nodded and said: "OK, yes. I can understand you did that. Sure, let him feel how hurt and angry you are. But my darling, if you love him and I'm sure you do, don't let it go on for too long. There is no point in antagonizing him."

No, Emma thought. I don't want to antagonize him. Marjorie was right. I still love him and I don't want to provoke him into doing something I will regret.

Sighing, she tossed the covers away from her and swung her legs over the edge of the bed. Putting on her dressing gown she went to the top of the stairs listening for noises. But all was quiet. Frowning she wondered where he was, and if he'd had his breakfast and his shower and had already left for work. The urge to look in the guest bedroom was great but she didn't.

He had spent most of the weekend in his study sometimes even closing the door and Emma wondered if he was trying to intimidate her shutting her out like she had shut him out. He had not really shown annoyance or anger but she knew he was angry. He was uncomfortable in her presence, especially at meal times. And what hadn't helped was, when at Saturday evening's dinner, Alan had opened one of his best wines to "celebrate your homecoming" and Emma telling him that while she appreciated the gesture he might have to drink most of it himself, as she'd had no alcohol during her stay in the hospital and didn't know how it would affect her. She should not have said that at least not so bluntly and disinterested. That had been insensitive and certainly had done nothing to break the tension.

For a moment Emma thought; Alan was going to smash the bottle on the table. His eyes flashed and for a long moment he sat perfectly still, then, calmly filling their glasses, he said: "It's good to have you back home."

Yes, Emma nodded pensively, she had been surprised to hear him say that considering the way he had been behaving. And again she asked herself, was she unreasonable shutting him out of their bed? Was she punishing him too harshly? But it had been such a shock when she had found out what he had been doing.

Emma remembered reading once in a novel; a woman saying to her husband when she found out he had been sleeping around. "I don't care how many women you fuck as long as you come back to me." Emma shook her head. She couldn't possibly think like that. That was not how she saw their marriage. She loved Alan, and she would never betray that love and she had expected the same from him. But he had betrayed that love and that was what was at the back of it all. The hurt and humiliation had gone deep and she just could not carry on as if nothing had happened. And he told her he loved her and I thought that he had said it more in the last month than in their entire marriage.

Even Marjorie had raised her eyebrows when she told her what she had done. Most of that evening's dinner had been eaten in silence and the atmosphere had been at best been awkward. After cleaning up Alan had gone to his study and closed the door. Emma had slept badly that night thinking about it all and trying to justify that what she had done was right. But Marjorie was also right when she said: "Don't push it. If you still want to have a life together."

Yes, Emma thought, I want to and hopefully a long life at that. More than ever now. She realized that she loved Alan and more than ever now did she feel a deep urge to put her arms around him and having part of him inside her, to be one with him. But what had she really wanted him to do? She asked herself, then she nodded. Yes, what she had really wanted had been for Alan to refuse to do, to argue with her, not accepting to go to the guest bedroom. She had wanted an argument when she could have told him what she thought of his behaviour. But he had said nothing. And it had felt that by not saying anything, he was trying to intimidate her.

Could that be the reason for Alan to accept her demand without protest? But he was angry. She was sure about that. Emma sighed, not much she could do about that now, not much she could do about anything now. However, what happened at Sunday evening dinner had given Emma some hope.

It had started rather awkwardly. Emma had put the wine glasses on the table but Alan had sat down without bringing a bottle. Ignoring Emma and the wine glasses Alan had started to eat.

Not knowing how he would react and bracing herself for the worst, Emma said: "Alan, please. I would like a glass of wine with my dinner. Would you mind?"

Alan had looked at her, got up and came back with a bottle of wine. Emma still remembered the look. It hadn't been exactly a friendly but more like a 'make up your bloody mind' look.

Emma shrugged. She couldn't blame him. After eating in silence for a while, which did nothing to ease the heavy atmosphere that surrounded them like an invisible blanket, and beginning to feel very upset and uncomfortable, Emma, in desperation and something to say said: "Alan, this is a lovely wine. Could you tell me please where it came from and what year?"

But all Emma could get, and rather suddenly, was: "Barossa Valley, 2007."

After some more time eating in silence Alan, not unfriendly, suddenly said: "Nice dinner Emma, thank you."

Taken completely by surprise, it took a few long moments before Emma was able to say: "Well, thank you, Alan. I'm glad you like it."

Encouraged by that Emma had asked him about his work but all he had answered to that was: "It's OK," and hadn't elaborated on that.

But towards the end of the dinner Alan had another surprise in store for her when he suddenly asked: "How do you feel now Emma? Is the wine affecting you?"

Emma had looked at Alan, trying to read sarcasm into it. But if it was meant as sarcasm he had hidden it very well. Then she had felt guilty thinking like that.

Emma went back to the bedroom, put on her dressing gown and went downstairs.

CHAPTER 37

Monday morning and Alan had meant to be on his way to work. Instead, he was standing at the kitchen bench, staring into nothing, every now and then shaking his head, sadly. It had not been good, the weekend. The high he had felt when taking Emma home had shattered, when she told him to sleep in the guest bedroom. He had been angry, a low smouldering anger that had engulfed his body and had lasted well into Sunday. When slowly in his mind he had begun to reason and understand the disappointment, frustration and anger he must have caused. In fact, thinking about it, it surprised him she hadn't kicked him out of the house altogether.

'You're a proper bastard,' he thought. 'I lied, I cheated and when she needed me I wasn't there for her. Too busy chasing after other women.' One of the things that came back to him most vividly was that morning on the balcony. Clenching his teeth he shook his head. How could he have been so insensitive? It had been haunting him ever since Emma had gone into hospital. He could see it, and what's more, feel it. Emma putting her arms around him, pressing into him, wanting love, but also, he had later realized, wanting his support and his help.

There was something else he remembered, which, at the time, he hadn't given a second thought. How thin she felt. Tears welled up in his eyes as he now fully comprehended how close he may have been at losing Emma. The thought was unbearable and now, more than ever, he realized how much she meant to him. There was something else too. Something that had been haunting him ever since they had come out of the hospital. It was the look she had given him when she opened her eyes. A look of sadness and rapprochement. A look that said: 'What have you done to me?' Alan cringed. Yes, what had he done to her? To his wife, to Emma, to the woman he loved more than life itself?

Incredulously he shook his head. 'He must have been out of his bloody mind.' He looked at his watch and sighed. Nearly 8 o'clock. He should have been on his way. He had wanted to, but somehow he couldn't, not without seeing Emma. He wanted to tell her how sorry he was and ask her to forgive him for what he had done to her.

Alan was just thinking whether she would listen to him and believe him, when his thoughts were interrupted.

When Emma entered the kitchen she saw Alan standing at the kitchen bench, staring out the window, the table set for breakfast. The drip coffee machine gurgling its water through the coffee grind, permeating the kitchen with the aroma of coffee.

Emma stopped, surprised and it took a few moments before she was able to say: "Oh, Alan, I didn't expect you to be still here."

Emma's surprise was genuine. She really had not expected Alan to be at home, not after a weekend of avoiding her and a behaviour that had sometimes bordered on rudeness. It had saddened her deeply because this was not what she had expected Alan to do. If he loved her so much, as he so often told her, and if he wanted to win her back, he wouldn't carry on like that and she certainly wasn't going to give in to that. But she missed him. His touch, his lovemaking and how he could make her feel wanted. But it had to be up to Alan to make the first move to reconciliation. And even then it would take time before she could completely give herself. Trust between them had been broken and this needed time to heal.

Upon hearing Emma's voice Alan turned around and in a subdued and apologetic voice said: "Good morning Emma. Yes, I am still here. I didn't want to go, not without telling you how sorry I am. Not only for how I have treated you but also for my inexcusable behaviours over the weekend. Please forgive me. I – er – well, I thought we – er – we could have breakfast together, that is, er – if you don't mind looking at me?" For a few moments there was absolute quiet. The air permeated with the aroma of coffee, hung heavily, when Emma, breaking the silence, carefully keeping emotion out of her voice, said: "Yes, OK. I will have breakfast with you."

This was more than she had expected. She would forgive him. She knew she would. Her love for him was too strong to let this come between them. But she had wanted Alan to make the first move. And he had. The reconciliation had begun.

www.ingramcontent.com/pod-product-compliance
Lightning Source LLC
Chambersburg PA
CBHW072144270326
41931CB00010B/1885